M000304101

The

PLAYSKOOL

Guide to Potty Training

The Best Strategies, Essential Information, and Practical Advice for Your Toddler's Potty Success

Karen Deerwester

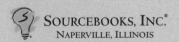

SOURCEBOOKS, INC.®
NAPERVILLE, ILLINOIS

Published by Sourcebooks, Inc.
P.O. Box 4410, Naperville, Illinois 60567–4410
(630) 961–3900
Fax: (630) 961–2168
www.sourcebooks.com

Library of Congress Cataloging-in-Publication Data
Deerwester, Karen.
  The Playskool potty training guide / by Karen Deerwester.
     p. cm.

  1. Toilet training. I. Title. II. Title: Potty training guide.
HQ770.5.D438 2007
649.'62—dc22

                              2007022270

Printed and bound in Canada.
WC 10 9 8 7 6 5 4 3 2

Dedicated to parents everywhere
who celebrate the value of play.
And to Jackson Quoc Bao, Shane Viet Dung, and Belly Baby!

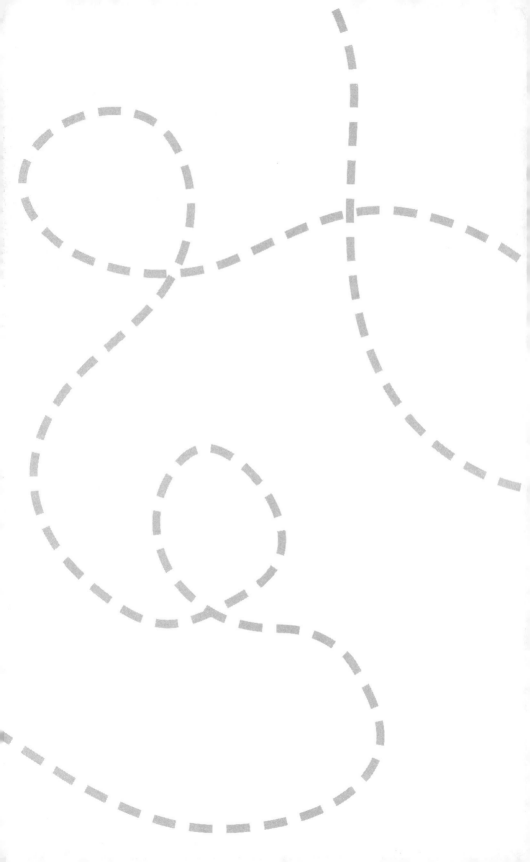

Acknowledgments

My work is play. I am grateful to all the people and places that encourage me to play on a regular basis.

To all the parents who attend my classes, who talk to me about their children, and who are willing to get silly with me, you make it all fun.

To everyone at the Ruth and Edward Taubman Early Childhood Center and at B'nai Torah Congregation of Boca Raton, Florida, who encourage playful noise and organized chaos; you spread joy.

To those who remind me each month that writing is play—Vicki from *South Florida Parenting Magazine*, Maria from *Blue Suit Mom*, and Linda and Liz from *The Boca Raton Observer*, you make the words dance on the pages.

To Peter Lynch and Shana Drehs from Sourcebooks, who agreed that potty training was play, you give ideas a playground. And to Sara Appino who edited the manuscript, you made perfect sense of my words.

To my friends who laugh with me and who humor me, you are my happy place.

To my family, you are the smile in my heart.

And to Richard, who reminds me what really matters in life.

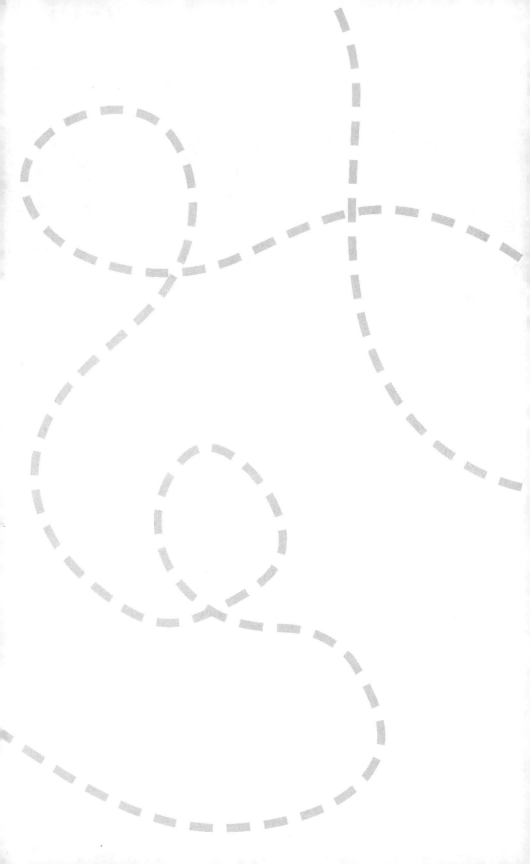

Contents

Introduction

Welcome to playful potty training. Playful potty training uses the language of childhood, *play*, as the foundation of potty training. Connect with your child through play. Teach your child potty skills and potty problem solving through play. Celebrate your child's personal style and potty training journey through play.

Play Is the Way

Playful potty training is the opportunity to have a fun potty partnership with your child and a time to celebrate his growing skills and interests. It is not a tedious, frustrating chore that has you wanting to run away from home until your child is happily wearing underwear with pink polka dots or blue dinosaurs. Your child is too smart for that. Playful potty training invites your child to join the club of happy potty goers at the time that's just right for him. He isn't a passive learner—he is taking charge of his body and his needs, with your helpful guidance and a variety of imaginative potty training strategies.

Potty training is a complex developmental puzzle. Your child needs you to help him put the pieces of the puzzle together. Sure, there will be challenges, because each child is unique. Each child's potty experience is based on what he knows, what he feels, what he likes, and how he learns best. But your child can accomplish anything with a playful partner, a playful attitude, and a positive playful environment. Your child learns best through play, the universal language of children.

Sometimes the pressure to potty train overshadows a child's developmental needs. Development matters. Caterpillars become butterflies, in good time. You would never throw a caterpillar into the air and yell, "fly!" And so it is with potty training. Some developmental components require time and nurturing, like giving a little caterpillar food and protection to grow. Playful potty training creates a similar nurturing environment that allows children to cross the bridge from the world of diapers to the world of underwear. This approach succeeds because it works hand-in-hand with your child's developmental strengths—not against them. Your child wants to grow. Your child likes being smart, strong, brave, curious, and resourceful. Your child wants to learn to use a potty. He just needs someone to lead the way. He needs someone to let him in on the secrets of the potty-goers club. And he needs help figuring out what he knows, what he feels, what he wants, and what he can do.

> Some potty training situations require more creativity than others, and some children need more support than others. Focus on your child—he's not wrong just because he's not responding the "right" way.

This book will show you how to make potty training meaningful and understandable to your potty-age child. It will help you understand your child's unique potty timeline, whether it's short or whether it's long, whether it begins closer to his second birthday or closer to his third birthday. Playful potty training is not a one-size-fits-all potty schedule. Playful potty training emerges from clear insights into your child's potty perspective that will inspire many happy potty adventures. It will help you to be realistic in your potty expectations and to be well prepared to handle any potty situation that arises. You will learn how to immerse your child in a natural, fun pottying environment.

Playful potty training consists of three stress-free phases. The first is *playful preparation*, a time to immerse your child in a positive learning environment. In this phase, you have no specific expectations for potty success. You happily engage your child in the natural world of pottying with an appreciation for his interest and abilities. The second phase is *potty play days*, a time to practice all the facets of potty-going in a supportive, playful routine. Potty play days are the active learning times when your child attempts to incorporate new potty skills while negotiating the distractions of daily life. By designating potty play days, you also make yourself available for support and encouragement. And finally, potty training includes a third phase, called *all day, all night*, to help your child adapt his potty play day skills to ever-changing potty situations. This phase includes night time pottying, potty accidents, and potty fears.

Potty training is about your child learning and growing. It works best when it's child-centered. It's time to go into your child's world of magical thinking and imaginative powers. Tap all those playful resources and more. Lead your child happily and willingly into a bigger world of underwear and bathrooms, flushing toilets, and independence. And if you lose your sense of fun, take a step back. Catch your breath. And remember, play is the way.

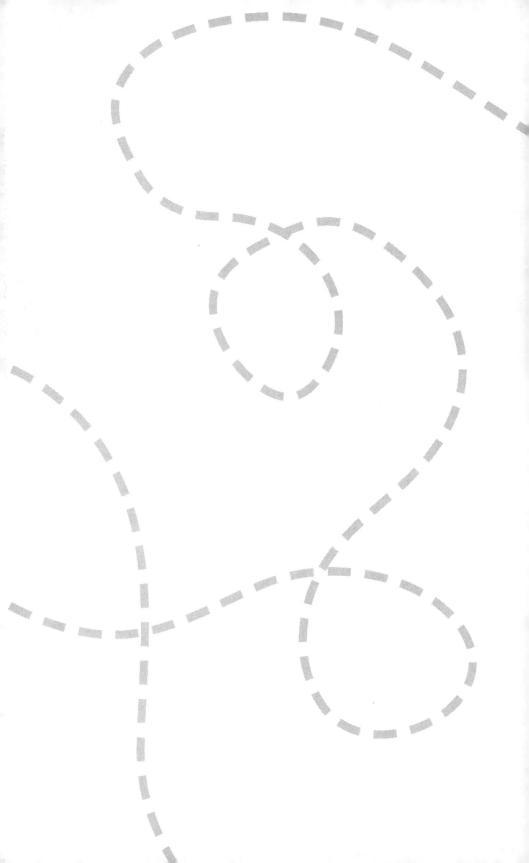

Part One

Playful Preparation

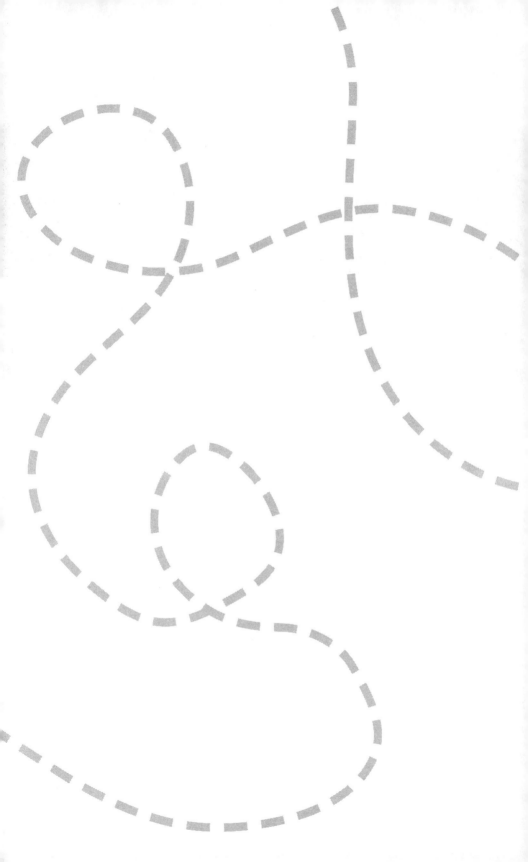

The Power of Playfulness

Play is the foundation of knowledge for your child. When she plays, she learns about her world in a meaningful and lasting way that is best suited to her developmental needs. Instinctively, she internalizes important concepts and skills and begins to define the kind of person she will become. She discovers right from wrong, the power of purposeful choices, and that success is a process. When she plays, your child is the director, making the connections that are most meaningful to her, rather than being shown or told the "right" connections by someone else. Learning happens naturally through play.

The Advantages of Playful Learning

Play is always more than what first meets the eye; it conceals an elaborate web of cognitive and emotional connections. Through the adventures of play, your child personally engages her whole world (or at least her day-to-day world). Simple games of hide-n-seek teach her that the world continues to exist even when people and things are shuffled around into new places.

That playful knowledge helps her to sleep better, knowing it's safe to close her eyes at bedtime. Filling and spilling buckets in the sandbox or cups in the bathtub helps her to comprehend and verbalize concepts of *full* and *empty*. Believe it or not, your child will later use these concepts to understand sensations in her potty-learning body.

Since child-logic is very different from rational adult-logic, learning is different for young children. Hands-on, multisensory, playful interaction with people and things is the best way to map new knowledge and new skills onto a child's growing brain. When your child's curiosity leads the way, she finds the answers to all *her* questions. Each child brings originality to learning and to potty training. Play develops your child's thinking—helping her think in new, unpredictable contexts—and enhances her self-esteem as a unique person.

Self-esteem grows from your child's interactions with the world. It is her tried and true belief in herself: "I can do this." Playful learning gives your child the opportunity for trial-and-error and for repeated practice. It allows her to safely stretch her abilities until the new abilities become automatic. When she experiences the "click" of learning, there's no turning back. It's as if she knew it all along! You see it in your child's glowing face. "I did it! I got it!" Mastery in a variety of situations under a variety of conditions gives your child the confidence to know she's ready for anything. Confidence and competence are not optional by-products of successful potty training; they are essential to the potty training process.

Play also strengthens the relationship between parent and child. Your child *needs* you to join in child-centered activities. Families who play together understand one another's strengths and struggles. They are better equipped to help one another with real-life problems, large and small. They also build a legacy of unconditional love and support. Play is the perfect foundation for potty training.

Playful Potty Training

With a few playful strategies, you can make potty training fun while you work on something you "have" to do anyway. If you can incorporate your child's natural interests and your child's developmental strengths into the learning process, the two of you might actually enjoy potty training. What's more, you might actually become an unbeatable team for life!

Which developmental accomplishments came first for your child? Walking or talking? Is your child a "natural" with people or with puzzles? When you approach potty training from a developmental perspective, there are no tests and no failures. Instead you open a window of endless possibilities, a window to fun and learning. You will immerse your child in a positive potty environment where pottying without diapers is a normal part of growing. You'll create fun

> If potty training feels like a battle, it's wrong for your child. Remember, parents always lose power struggles because the rules of engagement pit parent against child. If you feel a power struggle brewing, quickly call for an emotional truce. Give yourself a momentary time-out to regroup or consider a large scale reevaluation of your plan.

language and routines that give her positive messages about her body and her abilities. You'll watch—and wait—for her readiness signals while providing gentle support and encouragement.

Before you go any farther, think about the unique characteristics of your child. Which kinds of things come easily to her, and which require more time? Is she more active or more thoughtful? Does she prefer new experiences or familiar routines? Does she like doing things independently or with a buddy? Then, look at potty training from her point of view. What does she already know about the potty? Where are the missing links? And what could be the stubborn kinks? Consider your child's various developmental areas: her understanding of her body, her way of thinking, her linguistic ability, her social self, and her emotional self. You will be better able to support, encourage, and inspire your child if you try to see potty training from her point of view.

Your Child's Point of View

Your child already knows something about potty training. As you read about the different areas of development, you will discover that your child's strengths are already shaping her connections to potty training. This is your child's unique foundation for potty success. You will probably also discover a few missing elements, the developmental connections that your child has not made yet. These will be the road signs that guide you from where your child "is" to where your child "is going."

Your Child's Body

Children tune into their bodies in different ways. Your child might realize that the poop and pee are regular daily occurrences for everyone. She might make a connection between her body and pottying only after the fact that *she* pooped or peed. She might be able to identify that feeling in her body before she actually goes poop or pee, and do a potty dance letting you know that something is coming. Your child must read her body signals in order to become a successful pottygoer. She must also make a choice to not potty in the diaper. She needs to have the muscle control to hold the pee or poop until she can scurry to the nearest potty.

Yikes, that's a lot to do! Feel it…Hold it…Release it! The good news is that your child will make the body-potty connection at exactly the right time for her. Her personal potty training can be custom-designed to give her mastery over her body in the precise way that meets her needs.

Your Child's Thinking

Your child's potty thinking is what translates that physical body-potty connection into logical concepts. "*If* I don't like a wet diaper, *then* I can sit on the potty *before* I pee in my diaper." Or, "I *know* what that physical feeling means inside my body, and I need to *stop* what I'm doing for a few minutes to take a potty break. I *know* I can come back to what I was doing and *start again* in exactly the *same place.*"

These are complex concepts about time, sequence, predictability, cause, and effect. As an adult, you take all of these concepts for granted because you've been thinking like an adult for decades. Your potty-training-age child does not think like a miniature adult; she believes in fairy dust and dinosaur bones in the sand. The best way to potty train combines the simplest child-logic with a little magical flare that gives your child the power and conviction of success.

Your Child's Language

Language is a powerful tool in potty training. Putting experiences into words gives your child the ability to plan, to problem solve, and to ask for help. From the first "yes, I need to pee" to the more complex "I don't want to potty. It hurts to poop," potty training is easier when thoughts and actions can be put into the right words.

The right words—there's something to talk about. Your child may be talking up

> **As your child becomes interested in language, use these opportunities to familiarize her with potty language. Explain that you're changing her diaper because it's wet or because there's a poop.**

a storm, but finding the appropriate words to convey her ideas is another very complex skill. Just think about the last time a friend tried to give you unsolicited advice about how to improve the quality of your parenting. Was your first response the most clear, thoughtful, and effective one?

Potty training is infinitely easier when your child is able to follow verbal directions, discuss immediate and far reaching potty concerns, collect information in stories and songs, and verbalize emotions. But she can't do this without your help. Your goal is to find the right words to convey child-size bits of information, to say just enough without overwhelming or overtalking.

Your Child's Social Self

Becoming potty trained is like joining a new club of potty-goers. Your potty training child begins to identify herself with all her special role models: mom, dad, older brothers and sisters, peers, and friends. She is changing her self-image, letting go of some of the old, familiar baby ways. She also realizes that other people are watching her and have expectations for how she should act. They react to her choices with applause and appreciation or with disapproval and dismay. Social interactions inevitably influence your child's potty training experience.

Potty training should be a time of positive engagement and relationship building. It should not be a time of negative button-pushing and avoidance. Potty training takes you and your child into a new world of learning. There will be mistakes and sometimes emotionally volatile situations. Try to focus more on building a positive relationship with your child than on some right way of being successful. Your child will make the transition in her own time. You won't need to embarrass or humiliate her into giving up those familiar diapers.

Your Child's Emotional Self

Your potty-age child is exploding with emotional growth as much as she's growing physically. With every new shoe size, she probably learns a handful of new emotions—excitement, eagerness, fear, confusion, uncertainty, anxiety, pride, confidence, embarrassment, regret. With each new day, she discovers new ways things work and new points of view. In her increasingly complex child-world, new ways of thinking lead to new ways of feeling.

During potty training, your child is moving out of a perfectly protected baby world into the world of a child. She begins to learn that life doesn't always happen as planned, that learning new things involves age-appropriate risks, and that her feelings often make things easier or harder. In potty training, your child comes face-to-face with some difficult emotions, such as frustration, fear, or confusion.

This can lead to highly charged emotional situations. In potty training, you and your child directly or indirectly negotiate issues of control—often resulting in potty power struggles. You want to avoid or rethink any situation that turns potty training into a battle of wills, which can happen any time your way is different from your child's way. Playful potty training gives your child age-appropriate control of her potty choices and puts you in a position of support and guidance—not opposition.

Fun Means Child-Centered
- -

If you look at potty training from your child's perspective, you can approach potty training as just one of many childhood adventures. Your child wants to believe she is capable and smart, and she wants to have fun. Yes, potty training has its challenges. But challenges become opportunities when you focus on making this a positive experience for your child. They are opportunities for learning, opportunities for creativity, and opportunities for building a strong, supportive relationship.

Positive, playful, child-centered potty training requires faith in your child as a learner. Have faith in her—she will absolutely succeed at potty training one day. But she won't succeed according to another child's schedule or another person's expectations. She will succeed her way. Use fun to your advantage and create a happier potty experience that is focused on your child. Potty training isn't really about the potty anyway. It's all about your child!

- Your child makes a personal leap of faith every time she tries something new.
- Your child can say goodbye to diapers when she feels safe and confident with change.
- Your child has to make a deliberate choice about that physical sensation that she might need to pee or poop.
- Your child relies on her body, mind, and will to cooperate to reach the same desired goal.
- Your child has the final say about her own body, so power struggles will always be detrimental to a positive potty experience.
- Your child is still young enough to misjudge a sequence of events, to under- or overestimate the time needed to accomplish a task, or to get completely thrown off course by inconsequential circumstances.
- Your child needs a hand to hold when she's uncertain and needs someone to show her the way around tricky situations.
- Your child is learning how other people react to her mistakes and accidents.
- Your child needs a "potty partner" to make potty learning fun and funny.
- Your child needs you to give her a strong foundation on which you can grow and learn together for years to come.

2

A Playful Attitude

A playful attitude is one that is focused on the moment. Read your child's face. Listen to your child's questions. Go where your child needs to take you. You will be amazed at your ingenuity. A playful attitude is a well that never runs dry.

What Kind of Playful Are You?

Playful potty training looks different in different households. Find the kind of "playful" that works for you. Just as your child is a unique individual, so are you. Some parents are naturally goofy. Others are quietly silly. All parents know the joy of being with their own children, particularly when the stress and pressure of everyday life is locked far, far

> Potty training should be fun, as your child learns through play. Giggles always improve your chances of success.

away. Be yourself. Enjoy yourself. Sing, dance, create rhymes and tongue twisters, make faces, jump up and down and twirl around, make up guessing games.

Rediscover your inner clown. Are you slip-on-a-banana-peel funny? Ready for a pratfall or pretending your feet are glued to the floor? Are you "word" funny? Ready to dazzle your child with a song filled with a long list of rhyming words and nonsense words? Maybe you are a magician—able to do the impossible and the illogical, like move mountains and chase away monsters. Or create funny new worlds—animals that talk and creatures that dance in the trees. The secret is to surprise your child with the unexpected and to be a role model for imagination and new possibilities.

You don't have to sing embarrassing potty songs if that's not your style. You *do* have to believe that potty training will be fun. It's your job to invite your child into the potty-goers club by showing him that it's a happy place, not a fearful place. Saying goodbye to diapers is not just a must-do but a want-to-do. Your playful attitude creates a bridge of trust for your child to cross into unfamiliar territory.

First, let's try to eliminate a few potty training attitude busters. What are *your* deepest potty training fears?

Common Potty Training Fears for Parents

- My child will wear diapers to kindergarten. Or to college!
- My child will be the last child in town to potty train.
- People will think I'm a bad parent.
- I worry I'm doing something terribly wrong.
- My child will refuse to potty train just to spite me.

Do you hear whispers of something you'd like to avoid in this whole potty training experience? It's going to be very hard to be playful when you're trying to sweep your own doubts under the carpet. Trust yourself. Trust your child. Potty training really can be fun.

Why It Works

Rest assured that playful potty training gives you the ability to face your potty training anxiety. You will have the resources to address late potty-goers because you are working with your child's developmental strengths, which are increasing every year. Playful potty training is respectful and supportive of your child, so he is less likely to wage a war of resistance. You as a parent will also feel less stressed and have less self-doubt because you are focusing on relationship-building with your child instead of doing something *to* your child. Your best source of parenting is being "in the moment" with your child. Once you feel that bond, you too will be immune to the worries and doubt.

Playful potty training starts with a very pragmatic choice: the choice to keep moving forward at your child's pace. This pragmatic choice is based on accepting what you can and cannot control in potty training and making the best of it. You cannot force your child to potty where you want him to potty. Pushing him to potty train at your pace is likely to increase your child's resistance. Success isn't really success if he is anxious or confused. Keep your playful, child-centered attitude. Potty training will be a positive experience for you and your child, and you'll both be better problem solvers.

Playful Attitude = Greater Success

Success at any price is not success at all. Potty training is one of many developmental situations that will influence your child's confidence and competence in future learning. You want him to grow with a sense of personal mastery. "I did it! Hooray for me!" A playful attitude honors your child's experiences as a normal stage of development—there's no shame and no blame. There's no rush, either. Your child is growing just fine.

With a playful attitude, you recognize that your child—not you—is in control of significant pieces of the potty training puzzle, and his ability to stay dry doesn't happen on someone else's schedule. This helps you avoid the emotional landmines of potty training and ensures greater success. Because playful parents are not overly vested in "my way" or the "right way," they can invite their children to enjoy potty training as a new adventure.

Playful Attitude = Higher Self-Esteem

Your potty training age child may be experimenting with new emotional situations. This is an age for him to "test" the boundaries ("I wonder if mom means what she says?"). It's also the age for new fears ("Help! There's a monster in my closet!"). These new emotions add an extra dimension to potty training that takes time to explore. It will always be time well spent because it's time helping your child to grow into a healthy, happy person.

Your child's self-esteem is based on successful mastery of challenging situations, such as conquering his fears, managing mistakes, and taking risks in new environments. He learns that he is capable. He also sees his self-worth reflected in the opinions of the people he loves. He feels loved and accepted when he makes mistakes. And he feels supported until he can accomplish this important developmental landmark on his own. Playful potty training emphasizes your relationship with your child as

Tips for Boosting Self-Esteem
- Don't push for results when essential readiness components aren't in place yet.
- Acknowledge your child's idiosyncratic potty fears.
- Accept potty accidents.
- Keep the pressure off.

critical to building healthy self-esteem. Avoid the high personal cost of stressful potty training by concentrating your efforts on the ultimate, lifelong lessons to be learned from potty training.

Playful Attitude = Resourceful Problem Solving

Children learn problem-solving strategies directly from their problem-solving role models. If you teach potty training with a playful attitude, you claim your right to be flexible, creative, and resourceful. You learn to improvise. A fun, child-centered approach is the opposite of one-size-fits-all potty training. It is a custom fit for a particular child in your particular family at a particular moment in time.

The world doesn't stop while your child is potty training. You will juggle the demands of working, your child's transitions into playgroups and preschools, and a variety of family situations. Your child will be watching you every step of the way. How do you act when you are frustrated? What do you do when there isn't enough time to do everything you want to do? How do you ask for help when you need it? Playful potty training reminds you to persistently work toward a goal while keeping things fun and flexible along the way. The creativity and improvisation of playful potty training will help you both learn to be better problem solvers.

You will find many playful suggestions in the chapters ahead: games, songs, stories, routines, and rituals. If you maintain your playful stance throughout your personal potty adventure, you'll discover many more playful ideas of your own.

Understanding Your Child's Temperament

Temperament affects how you learn and how you handle change. It also affects potty training. Your child was born with a temperament style that was evident within the first twenty-four hours and that will be there when he goes to off to college. After all, your personal temperament style that was on full display as a child is still in you today as a parent. Luckily, you have had many years to learn to compensate for times when your temperament makes situations more challenging.

Nearly four decades ago, acclaimed child researchers Stella Chess and Alexander Thomas identified three primary temperament styles in children: easy, slow-to-warm-up, and difficult. Each temperament style has strengths and weaknesses. The "easy child" may be flexible and open to new situations but may not tell you forcefully if he experiences physical discomfort. This child is not necessarily happier than the other temperaments, he just won't create a scene over nothing. The "difficult child" does not have an intrinsic flaw. He is just being intense as he doggedly pursues his agenda and protests forcefully if you don't understand. The "slow-to-warm-up child" always takes his time to observe and grow into new situations.

> Understanding your child's temperament helps you shape realistic potty expectations and discover playful strategies that work best for your child. You will find clues to the pace of potty training, the amount of energy required, and the kinds of games that support your child's mastery. Understanding temperament helps you eliminate that highly stressful potty training question—"Why is my child different?"

Parents usually see aspects of different temperament styles in each individual child.

Some combinations of temperament styles can sound counter-intuitive. For example, your child might be "easy" and "difficult" at the same time. He might enjoy new people and places, and be the first to join a group. Yet when he falls apart, he does so with shocking fury. This happens consistently, whether he is an infant or in his "terrible twos."

Or, your child might be slow-to-warm-up and difficult. He could be the happiest kid on the block at home where the routine is consistent and predictable. But when faced with a new situation, he may need slow, frequent repetition. And if he gets frustrated, he loses the ability to stand back and regroup. Instead he shouts an earth shattering "NO!" and runs to the farthest reaches of the house.

The important message behind the research on temperament styles is that adults can modify their parenting styles to better complement an individual child's strengths. Will your child eagerly want to potty in every new bathroom in town or will your child want time to analyze every nuance of each new potty experience? Will a silly potty song help your child to relax on the potty or will it make him angry because he doesn't want to be there at all?

The best potty training practices will take into account different temperaments and will work most of the time. Visualize your child's likes and dislikes as you gather a little bag of parenting tricks that fits your child's unique personality. Playful potty training is being prepared to meet your child exactly where he is today.

Easy Temperament

The child with an easy temperament is usually the easiest to potty train. But *easy* does not mean *automatic*. Each temperament brings strengths and challenges to the potty learning experience.

Characteristics of an easy temperament:

- He is less frenetic and able to sit for short lengths of time.
- He adapts well to schedules. Feeding schedules and nap schedules are predictable, which also leads to a predictable pottying schedule.
- He isn't easily distracted from a task. If he sees a new toy on his way to the bathroom, he will remember to come back to it after he goes potty.

- He can listen to verbal encouragement and support without a strong emotional reaction.
- The sensory experience of sitting on a cold potty or of a naked bottom is not overwhelming.
- He will respond easily to pottying in a variety of situations under a variety of conditions. He is more likely to pause one activity if he needs to take a potty break.
- His frustration may be expressed more mildly. Mistakes and setbacks will be small blips on the way to success, rather than major pitfalls.
- He may be eager to embrace new potty expectations, such as sitting on a new potty. He may even claim to be ready before physical readiness is apparent.
- Overall, the potty process is more likely to be light-hearted. You may experience quick success or steady progress instead of an emotional roller coaster.

Of course, there are also unique challenges to potty training a child with an easy temperament. He may not care if he needs a clean diaper. He is not distressed by the minor inconveniences of diapers. The motto "life is good" was written for him.

The child with an easy temperament may not ask to be potty trained. If you ask him to use a potty, he will. But if you don't ask him, he's equally content. And if you're a busy parent, you might be relieved that he doesn't seem to need you. As a result, this child could be the last to be potty trained. In this case, if you hear your inner voice asking "Hmmmm, I wonder if he's ready?" it may be time to take a few simple steps to gently move your child forward into the next stage. You may be happily surprised at the easy results.

Difficult Temperament

The child with a difficult temperament probably won't potty train without some concentrated effort. This child likes things "his way" but will respond to clear expectations and attentive support.

Characteristics of a difficult temperament:

- Potty training is a physical activity to this child. He may not love sitting still but he may love running to the potty or pulling the toilet paper when he's finished. You can give timely reminders to keep your child's activity level focused—"First potty, then we'll pull this much toilet paper...and STOP." Teaching "stop" is a game, not a threat.
- His schedule can be unpredictable, which is a strength if you are a flexible parent. You may need to check in on his needs rather than expect today to resemble yesterday.
- Attention from adults is extremely important. Your genuine engagement outweighs any other distraction and will be a powerful resource while potty training this child.
- He likes to do things in a big way. Use this trait to create big potty training excitement.
- He will experience every nuance of the potty training experience. If you tune-in to his sensory world, you can make the necessary adjustments and give him explicit verbal descriptions of his feelings.
- He likes to feel in control. You can turn this into a positive by letting him feel like he's choosing where, when, and how to potty. Of course, you must remain the invisible hand orchestrating his success.
- He hates to give up. Use this as a potty training strength by focusing on the small successes that bring your child closer to ultimate success.
- He will vehemently protest change. You can honor this child's voice—say it loud and say it strong—without you, the parent, collapsing in self-doubt.
- He may say "NO!" when he really means "maybe." He also wants to wear underpants one day. The world is full of brilliant high-maintenance people—artists, scientists, inventors. You will have great stories to tell and possibly develop a great sense of humor along the way.

The child with a difficult temperament will likely be the most challenging to potty train. But remember, this is not about you as the parent doing things wrong and it's not about the child deliberating making your life stressful. This is about the way your child approaches new situations. This is how he was born.

You cannot change a child's temperament. You can, however, teach your child to make the most of his strengths. He can learn how he will respond in different situations and will eventually learn successful strategies to compensate for challenging moments.

This requires time and energy on your part, especially during the potty training years. Your child needs you to help him regulate experiences until he learns self-control. He is stuck wanting control and hating change—stuck between too much and too little. It's up to you to build the bridge that will take him across.

Because this child resists change, he may not feel "ready" for potty training. You will have to observe readiness characteristics on your own and start building that bridge. You may have to work hard to win his buy-in. But once you have it, he won't let anything stand in his way.

Slow-to-Warm-Up Temperament

The child with a slow-to-warm-up temperament can appear easy because of his quiet nature. He handles change well when it is introduced slowly, allowing him to gradually become comfortable and confident in new situations.

Characteristics of a slow-to-warm-up temperament:
- This child is often described as watchful. He likes to be prepared before taking action, which is a strong positive for potty training. He is the least impulsive of the three temperament styles.
- He likes to know what's happening next. His mild disposition complements the predictability of a potty training routine.
- He is the classic tortoise moving steadfastly toward a goal. It may take him longer, but he always gets there.
- You won't have loud power struggles with a child who has a

slow-to-warm-up temperament. This child voices opposition in less direct ways.

- He may seem very sensitive to the physical sensations of potty training. You can give him orienting cues of new sensations to ease his hesitancy. For example, he will think it's a game if you remind him to listen to the pee falling in the toilet.
- He likes learning new skills. He just needs to do it on his own time schedule. With adequate preparation, he does adapt.
- He tends to linger on the sidelines rather than jump forward with both feet (until you really get to know him, that is). The good news is you probably won't find him upturning potty chairs and running wildly through the park without his pants.
- His mood is more cautious rather than negative or positive. This will give you time to adjust your potty training to fit his needs.

Potty training a child with a slow-to-warm-up temperament can be exhausting if you don't want to revisit each step each and every day. This child loves repetition, so prepare yourself to work closely with his timetable. Because this child has a tendency to withdraw in new situations, he may withdraw instead of asking for help when he needs it. Don't jump in and rescue him. Simply remind him you are there to help if he asks.

This child also tends to register his unhappiness mildly. Therefore, he could get a little whiney. Let him know you are happy to help but he needs to ask for help in appropriate ways. Similarly, watch out for quiet subversion. In his attempt to buy more time, he can sabotage his own success.

The biggest obstacle to potty training a child with a slow-to-warm-up temperament is a spontaneous, impulsive parent. This child cannot be rushed, so take a deep breath and prepare to proceed slowly.

Your Temperament Matters, Too

Temperament styles are still very much part of your adult personality. You may have learned adaptive strategies to camouflage less effective temperament traits, but those traits are just under the surface and show up when you least expect. Your genuine temperament style comes out when you are most yourself with close friends and family.

Are you mostly an easygoing, adaptable, flexible, go-with-the-flow person? Would people describe you as even-tempered without a lot of peaks and valleys? When things go wrong, do you respond mildly and easily move on to the next thing?

Or, do you like to be well-prepared in new situations—do you rehearse speeches and practice skills many times in advance? Does it take others a little time to get to know the real you? Do you plan ahead what to wear to a new place and practice a few tried-and-true conversation starters or jokes to break the ice? Or do you like things "your way" and "now"? Would others describe you as meticulous or intense?

You want your expectations to match your child's temperament style. Otherwise, you're headed for a highly stressful potty training experience. If you and your child share a temperament style, you will intuitively know what to expect from your child. You will also already have an abundance of adaptive strategies to help your child be successful.

There is also the possibility that you wish your child did not have your temperament style. You may wish he were more assertive than cautious like you. Or, you may wish he would just let a problem go instead of dwelling on it for hours. Self-acceptance will serve you well here. You can also recruit potty partners who do not take your child's behaviors personally.

If you and your child have different temperament styles, you might approach your child with unrealistic assumptions. The parent with an easy temperament might grow exhausted by a child with a difficult temperament—it's not easy. The parent with a difficult temperament might approach potty training with more intensity than is warranted. The parent with a slow-to-warm-up temperament might still be thoroughly researching potty training long after the child is ready. You are who you are. Parenting gives you that incredible opportunity to learn about yourself as you learn about your child.

Keeping It Fun

Potty training can be a conundrum. You can face seemingly illogical questions, like "Why does my child ask to use the potty and then not go?" or "Why did my child regress after having so much initial success?" Temperament helps you to unravel the mysteries of your child's particular experience and proceed confidently toward creative solutions. Most importantly, temperament helps you put yourself in your child's shoes. Your child is not being obstinate or defiantly slow to drive you crazy. Your child is trying to learn a complex new skill in frequently confusing situations with only a few short years of experience in this world!

Relax, potty training can be fun. Honor your child's individuality. Choose strategies that make potty training easier—not harder—for your child. Realize that your attitude dictates the stress-o-meter. If you're having fun, your child will too. All you have to do is play.

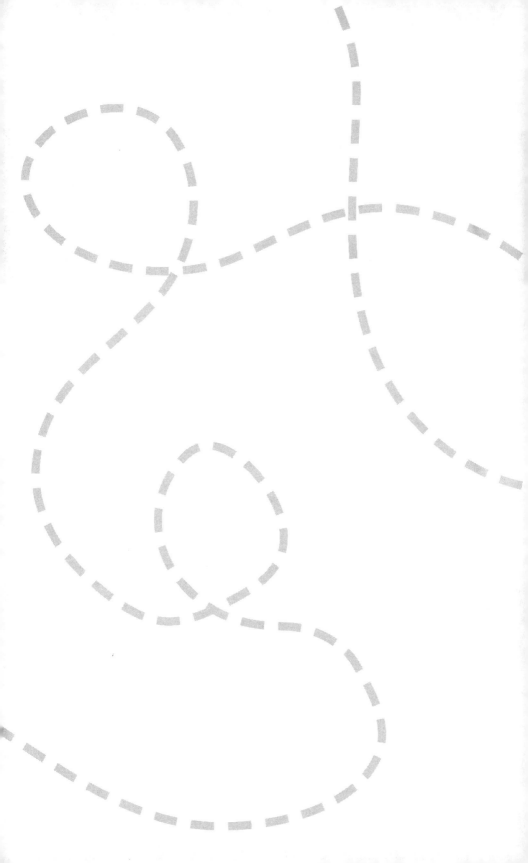

Playful Potty Training Readiness

3

Imagine your child is standing in front of a gate to an unknown castle full of riches. She's been given a very heavy key ring with five color-coded keys. Each key must fit into the correct lock for the gate to open. And your hands are too large to maneuver the keys for your child. She must do it herself.

In most cases it will take a little trial and error to unlock the gate. Sometimes all the keys fit, and your child hesitates to step through the gate because everything looks different. Every adventurer needs a faithful companion who believes in her. Your child needs your experienced potty training perspective to both lead the way through uncertainties and to follow obligingly when all is well.

Your child needs you to set realistic expectations for potty training. She needs you to guide her toward a shared goal. She needs you to help her solve problems in a variety of potty training situations. And she needs you be a partner that celebrates her successes and minimizes her struggles. You do this best when you understand the essential developmental ingredients to successful potty training.

Five Ingredients to Potty Training Readiness

The five ingredients to potty training readiness are your child's physical ability, your child's cognitive ability, your child's linguistic ability, your child's social ability, and your child's emotional ability. When these developmental potty factors come together—click, the gate opens.

- Physical ability: Your child can stay dry for short periods of time.
- Cognitive ability: Your child understands the sequence of before, during and after, as well as the big picture: "When I choose to use the potty, I'll say goodbye to my diapers."
- Linguistic ability: Your child can communicate the need to potty before she actually pees or poops.
- Social ability: Your child wants to join the potty goers club.
- Emotional ability: Your child is curious and motivated.

> While you can immerse your child in the natural experience of pottying, you cannot change when your child will acquire the physical control of actually peeing and pooping. That's one area of readiness where you have to sit back and wait.

Potty training is a snap when you have the five developmental ingredients in place. But individual child development can be a bit of a trickster. Your child might desperately want to wear fancy underwear but not have the slightest clue when she physically needs to potty. Or your child might love using the potty except if she's busy playing a game, when she could care less what happens.

A potty partner has two choices in these kinds of situations: sit back and wait for the emerging skill to appear—and it always does eventually—or try to create the optimal environment for that missing ingredient to flourish. If, for example, your child is missing the communication skills, you can model potty language and create helpful potty signals. If your child forgets about pottying when more exciting things are happening, you can establish consistent routines like taking a potty break before starting a new activity or before leaving the house. A few naked potty times may help a child make the physical connections. But in all cases, if *you're* doing most of the "work," it could be a sign to step back and wait for development.

Potty training is the whole deal. You need to be your child's potty partner until the day when all five of the readiness ingredients come together most of the time under most conditions. Slow-going potty training can frustrate a fast-going parent. Try not to focus on "when" and instead focus on "how" you can create a positive potty environment for as long as your child needs it. Remember, potty training is at your child's pace. Able doesn't always mean ready. Only your child can say when she's ready.

Observing Your Child

Before you actively start potty training, observe your child for cues when to begin. Look at her behavior in the different areas of development (body, thought, language, social self, and emotional self) for hints that she is ready to get started. Collect clues as to where she may need more time, more information, or more support. The following are typical behaviors that indicate a child is ready to begin potty training.

The Physical Behaviors:
- Your child stays dry for at least two hours during the day.
- Your child wakes up dry from naps.
- Your child will pee or poop regularly: before bath time, an hour after breakfast, etc.

- You see telltale signs when your child is pottying: she stops playing, makes a certain face, squats in a more private part of the room, etc.
- Your child can walk to a designated place to accomplish a goal.
- Your child can remove pieces of clothing to use the potty.

The Cognitive Behaviors:

- Your child is curious about how her body works.
- Your child sees the connection between her body and the potty.
- Your child understands sequencing: before, during, and after.
- Your child lines up her toys, understands order and things in "right" places.
- Your child thinks ahead: She can stop doing something if she needs to potty.
- Your child comprehends that potty books and videos are relevant to her actions at this time.
- Your child understands the big picture—"so *this* is how things work."

The Social Behaviors:

- Your child wants to follow others into the bathroom.
- Your child tries to imitate adult potty behavior.
- Your child enjoys helping others.
- Your child appreciates a good audience.

The Emotional Behaviors:

- Your child asks questions about pottying.
- Your child likes clean diapers and asks to be changed at appropriate times.
- Your child cares about the outcomes of her actions. She expresses likes or dislikes after she does something and, if reminded, will remember those preferences the next time.
- Your child is willing to sit still to master a task.

The Verbal Behaviors:

- Your child knows her body parts.
- Your child can tell you, first *when* she's pottied in her diaper, and then *before* she's pottied in her diaper.
- Your child follows simple directions: "Quick, run to the bathroom!"
- Your child tells you what she needs.
- Your child says she wants to "do it myself."

Promoting Potty Training Readiness

You can help fill in some of the missing pieces in the readiness puzzle as long as you follow your child's lead. Discover the excitement of potty training with your child. Use a gentle curiosity to explore what she knows and what she wants to know in each area of development.

Physical Readiness

Recognize when your child takes charge of her body. Notice when she pees or poops in her diaper and tell her that's what she's doing. You'll be adding to her awareness of what her body does.

Cognitive Readiness

Similarly, talking to your child about pottying may create a new cognitive awareness. You may be holding the missing link that she is looking for. Start with neutral descriptions of your behavior: "Wait here while mommy goes to the potty. I drank a lot of water today."

Linguistic Readiness

Add language to daily potty activities. Talk about what you're doing and ask your child engaging questions. Talking about pottying is just like asking her to point to the moon or tell you the color of the grass, an ordinary on-going conversation.

Social Readiness

Include your child in your bathroom routine. Again this is as natural as your child watching you talk on the phone and then imitating your behavior. Engage her in casual conversations about who uses the potty and who uses diapers. Let her draw her own conclusions about who, what, where, and when.

Emotional Readiness

Stay out of power struggles. Negative attention gives your child a strong incentive to delay potty training. Without pressure or competition, she makes the potty choices that feel right to her today. Trust and respect will lead her to embrace growth and change.

In every instance, however, give it up if your child looks bored. Wait for a better time when you can get positive feedback from your child. While you can immerse your child in the natural experience of pottying, you cannot determine when your child will acquire the physical control of actually peeing and pooping. That's one area of readiness where you have to sit back and wait. Be patient; there's still plenty to do for a ready-to-go positive potty partner, as you will see. Ready-to-go potty partners, also known as "trying not to rush" potty training parents, might want to post this daily reminder on their bathroom mirror: Early potty goers are in no way smarter or more advanced than later potty goers. Respect for individuality is a far greater gift.

Other Readiness Factors

Gender Differences

Girls may potty train earlier than boys but, if so, it's only a difference of a few months. Keep in mind that gender differences are statistical differences. They do not predict when your child is ready or when your child will be successful.

Toddler-age girls may have earlier language development. They can then verbalize the potty process and talk about the sequence of events with caregivers. Listening skills also help young children to follow directions better and to think before acting. With earlier language skills, children can communicate their immediate needs and recruit adult help in getting to the closest potty.

Toddler-age boys may be more active at physical play. Energetic boys may master control of their body and limbs but may not be as tuned into the inner workings of their bodies. They may not have the patience to sit for a few minutes on a potty and notice how they can control what comes out. Timing, of course, is everything. In every case, interest plus developmental landmarks will be the determining factors.

> If your child asks, "Am I wearing diapers or underpants?" in order to decide whether to potty or not, she is ready to say goodbye to diapers.

Early Starters

Your child between one-and-a-half and two years old may demonstrate an interest and an ability in potty training, particularly if she is not in an intense "no" stage. If you're both enjoying the time and the attention, this may lead to long-term success. It doesn't always. Often, the novelty of the experience wears off for one or both of you. Your child may not be ready to assume more responsibility for the potty experience for another six months or more. And you can become easily overwhelmed doing all the potty training "work." If this happens, continue your positive potty environment until you see the following signs. Then, active potty training will be easier for you and more meaningful for your child.

- Does your child actually feel the sensation of needing to go to the potty without your reminders?
- Is she willing to initiate a request for help if you forget to ask her?
- Does she really care about potty training or does she love potty training with you?

If you are not seeing the above mentioned signs, you can still support and encourage your child's progress toward happy potty training, but with far less stress.

Oppositional Stages

Potty training is more complicated when your child is in an oppositional stage. Oppositional stages can intensify counterproductive power struggles between you and your child, adding stress and delays to the potty process.

The first of these oppositional stages occurs when your child is around eighteen months of age, or the first time she says "No" and "Mine." In this stage, she is pushing away from you to become her own person. Every "no" challenges the world to acknowledge her. She feels powerful and likes the way it feels. "Mine" is her way of defining herself and her place in the world. She rules the world by making a claim on everything she touches.

Somewhere around two-and-a-half years old, you will witness another highly volatile stage. Your child will be experiencing a new set of highly charged emotions to complement new gains in language development. Your emerging little person is now confronted by fears, frustration, anger, and jealousy.

These stages trump all other learning because your child's emotional growth requires front-and-center status. Growth spurts usually create a temporary but necessary imbalance. Wait a few months for potty training and your cooperative child will return, ready to tackle new challenges with a renewed sense of strength.

Potty Training Babies

Potty training babies under one year of age is possible. It does, however, mean something different than the earlier description of potty training as an independent skill. Potty training children who are younger than one year old is an interdependent potty venture. The same interdependent philosophy is found in Suzuki music education, where the parent learns the instrument before the child so the parent can be a teaching partner.

Mom, or another caregiver, gets the baby to the potty at the right time and assists her in the potty process. This may work better with babies who do well on a schedule. Mom watches the baby for signals that she is ready to go, from grunts to wiggling. Mom carries the baby to the potty, adding a sign or signal of her own; for example, a psssing sound. In time, the baby associates the signal with pottying. Voila, no more diapers!

> People in many countries around the world, such as African countries, Japan, China, India, and many Latin American countries, potty train babies under one year of age. One way is not better than another. Successful potty training must fit your family's reality. Your job is to decide what will work in your household at this particular time for this particular child.

This process only works with time, attention, and a noncoercive loving partnership. It is not for the overworked and the overscheduled, and not in homes trying to juggle the needs of adults and other family members.

Early potty training has distinct advantages for the parents. The thrill of no more diapers to change is liberating. The financial savings of no more diapers is significant. And then there is the pride that your child has successfully mastered an important childhood landmark. Add an extra "wow" to that pride if your child is the first to be potty trained among her peers.

Does a child, let's say under the age of two, feel additional pride for beating her friends in the potty game? No, young children feel pride in what *they* can do; they don't compare themselves with others at this age. Children feel pride in mastering potty training whenever the time comes that they master potty training.

Children do look to parents and special adults for feedback on their successes. For that reason, you want to be sure that your parenting agenda is consistent with your child's developmental stage. Potty training before your child is ready can increase resistance and delay success. Keep in mind that early potty-goers are not more intelligent than their peers and sustain no long-term advantages.

Potty Training Twins or Multiple Same-Age Siblings

Even though children are born at the same time from the same parents, it does not mean they will have the same potty training schedule. Each child has a unique temperament style and his or her own personal developmental clock. You may have one child who is a potty natural, leading the way to easy, early success. Your other child may not be interested until months later. And when she is ready, her potty training style may be completely different than that of her sibling.

It is best not to assume both children will complete potty training at the exact same time. Try to form your expectations for each individual child by looking at his or her readiness traits separately. Create the same positive potty environment for both children, but plan on modifying your potty plan to meet each child's individual needs. One child may want to do everything by herself while the other wants your hands-on support. One might strongly dislike diapers while the other relishes the security.

However, there are advantages to potty training same-age siblings together. For example, they can learn from watching one another. A hesitant child sees the confidence of a bold child. A child who doesn't comprehend pieces in the potty process has her best friend there to show her. They help each other. They laugh together. They grow together. Enjoy potty training as a team, but remember everyone on the team has different strengths.

What to Do While You're Waiting for Readiness

Start pre-potty training when your child is between one-and-a-half and two years old. At this time of potty preparation, expect nothing from your child. You, on the other hand, can prepare the stage for potty training and fill in some of the positive potty scenery. You haven't written the script yet and you're still months away from potty training rehearsals, but there's plenty of work a parent can do to get ready now.

- Establish your positive potty training attitude.
- Choose your potty words.
- Include your child in your bathroom routines.
- Introduce a potty chair.
- Talk with your child about diapers and potty routines.
- Add a few potty books to your child's home library.
- Interview friends and colleagues about their potty training experiences.
- Casually observe potty behaviors of children six to twelve months older than your child.

As you practice your playful potty training attitude, watch your child's reaction to the new stimulus you are presenting. Stay with the basics until she expresses more curiosity. You immersed your child in language-rich experiences long before she started talking. The potty basics create a potty-rich environment long before active potty training, as you will see in the next chapter.

Soon enough you will notice your child is curious. She is initiating potty behavior: She wants to sit on her potty. She doesn't like wearing diapers. She likes the idea of doing things the way her sister does them. Follow your child's lead. Add a few potty visits to her daily schedule—have her sit on the potty chair after a nap if she has a dry diaper and after undressing before bath time. Make simple connections between her behavior and the potty. Say, "Look there's pee pee in the potty!" Or, just as effective, "Look there's no pee pee in the potty this time."

Do not assume at this point that she's ready to run the potty marathon. She has no idea what the potty marathon is yet. Start by explaining the big picture first. Explain that when she's a little older, she won't wear diapers anymore. Watch and listen. Is she as comfortable saying goodbye to diapers as she is ready to say hello to princess underpants? This is a time of exploration for your child and a time for you to evaluate how quickly or slowly to advance to the next level.

> Usually if children are busy mastering other physical milestones, they are not ready to move forward to a new one like potty training. Running and climbing usually precede pottying because they bring your child pure joy in and of themselves. Give your child time to enjoy physical movement before asking him to use those movements to meet other goals.

If it seems like your child is not anywhere near her peers in potty training, look at how she's doing in the areas of development: motor skills, language skills, cognitive skills, social skills, self-control, and emotional literacy. Potty training is one small part of overall development.

Your child may just not be ready when you're ready. In one possible scenario, your child may have a slow-to-warm-up temperament style that is cautious to the point of not being able to take that necessary step forward. Sometimes, you can give your child a gentle push to experience her long-awaited success.

Alternatively, you may be the person who isn't ready. By the time your child is three years old, you should be involved in some sort of supportive potty training. At a minimum, you will be creating a positive potty environment and establishing the foundation for future readiness.

Timing Is Everything

In a Western culture that stresses independence, "potty training" usually includes the entire process from understanding the first need-to-potty sensations to the after-potty self-help skills. A potty trained child feels the need to potty before pottying and is interested in controlling where and when she potties. She can communicate the need to potty and can physically hold it until she gets to a potty. She can remove the necessary clothes to go potty and can wipe herself afterwards.

This complete package called "potty trained" happens somewhere around three years old, with many children needing help wiping bowel movements until they are nearly four years old.

Some children will demonstrate all the potty training skills after their second or third birthday, while others will have a few of the key ingredients, but not all. The potty training process, from the time some of the necessary abilities emerge until the total package "clicks," can take six to eight months. However, this should not be six months of desperation. Rather, it is six months of moving toward self-reliance, while sometimes taking a few steps back.

The learning process leading up to that final finish line might be quick, or it might be slow. Just remember, the tortoise and the hare both get to the same goal. However, pushing the tortoise makes her retreat, not go faster.

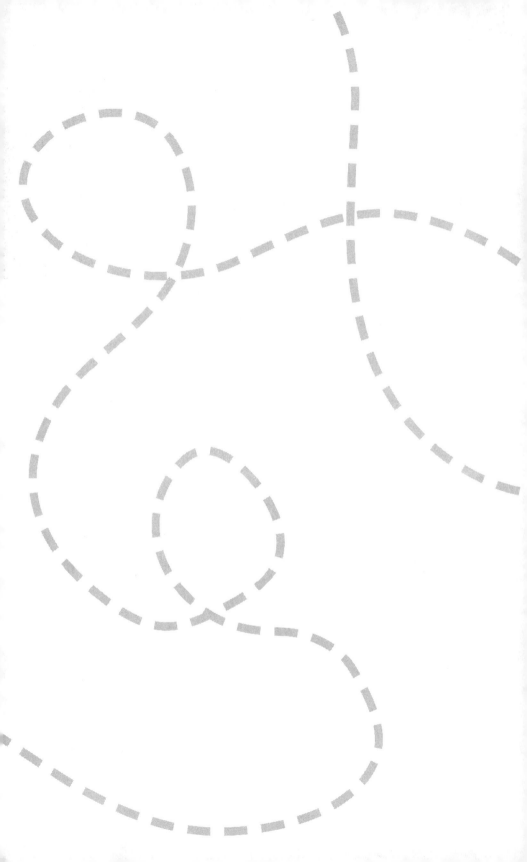

4

A Playful Potty Training Environment

Your child picks up clear messages from his environment. These messages can support or hinder your attempts at potty training. You want potty training time to be geared to your child's body, your child's way of thinking, and your child's needs. You create a playful potty training environment by creating a potty-friendly physical space and a child-friendly learning atmosphere.

Creating a Child-Centered Potty World

It's time to convert your former adult-using bathroom, or baby-using bathroom, into a child-size space for self-care. It's time to rethink your daily routine to make time for your child to take care of his own needs. You're now moving onto potty-standard-time. Remember how much longer it takes for your child to walk into the store by your side instead of gliding in a stroller or in your arms. Think of how much longer it takes when your child dresses himself. Visualize the mess and chaos of your child feeding himself. You are moving into a potty world that seems far more inefficient by adult standards, but less-than-perfect practice is the surest way to independence.

Play is the defining theme that measures whether your adaptations match your child's world. Since your child learns through play, giggles always improve your chances of success. You are modifying your home, your potty routines, and your daily schedules to create a child-centered potty world. Bathrooms become places to confidently learn new skills with child-friendly potty accessories. Day-to-day life temporarily shifts to accommodate changing potty needs. You are creating space and time for the upcoming potty adventure with all the new games and strategies you will be learning. The following are some characteristics of a positive potty environment.

- Bathrooms should be child-friendly. Your child does not want to spend time in a place he's told is dirty and disgusting.
- Routines should be stable and predictable. Your child is learning to pay attention to significant moments in his day. You can make that easier if your child can guess when those moments are most likely to happen.
- Schedules should be relaxed. Eliminate the frantic need to be in too many places at once. If you do, your child will have time to think.
- Expectations should be opportunities for success. Unrealistic demands and the threat of failure undermine the process of learning from mistakes.
- Choose easy-to-clean clothes and surfaces. Fancy clothes and new carpeting add to your frustration without adding anything to your child's learning.

A Happy Potty Place

Some children will happily potty anywhere, anytime. But to some children, a bathroom is a formidable place with big, hard fixtures and big, cold expectations. A positive bathroom environment will help your child feel at ease testing his early potty skills. A child-friendly bathroom gives your child the feeling this is *his* special place to grow and learn. As with all playful learning, your child is at the center of a very personal experience. Is the bathroom a happy place for your child? Create a positive space where he wants to spend valuable time learning.

You don't need a professionally decorated child-themed bathroom to entice your child. You definitely do not need expensive fixtures and accessories that have you hovering over your child's use. Think instead about what your child looks at when *he* sits on the potty. Would he like a mirror to see himself? Would he like to see a piece of his artwork framed or an enlarged picture of himself on the potty or of him washing his hands? Would he like a book basket nearby? Consider your potty room from your child's point of view and create a place of ease and comfort for him.

> **Reading may help your child sit on the potty longer. Keep a basket of books, catalogs, and old mail next to your child's potty, but also let your child know that potty reading is a means to an end and not an end in itself.**

- Write your child's name with a colorful permanent marker or add stickers to his potty chair or his step stool.
- Add theme towels or personalized name towels. Decorate your own with fabric paints or buy your child's favorites.
- Use child-friendly hooks for your child's towel instead of the usual towel bar.
- Add some fun foam soap in an attractive child-pump dispenser.
- Create a pull-up/dry clothes station where your child can change during the transitional weeks. Designate a drawer or add a cubby for clean pull-ups.
- Double check that the temperature on the hot water is turned down.
- Use an easy wash enamel-base paint on the walls.

Even though your child is becoming more independent in his

potty exploration, continue to supervise when he's in the bathroom for safety and positive potty habits.

If your home has more than one bathroom, designate one as your child's special potty place, preferably a bathroom close to where he plays or sleeps. This may pose a problem if you live in a two-story house. If so, pick the bathroom that has easiest access for a potty training child in a hurry. You also have the option of buying multiple potty chairs or potty seats for multiple bathrooms.

The Potty Chair or Potty Seat

Before you begin any structured potty training, introduce your child to the potty furniture. Potty chairs and potty seats come in many varieties, from minimalist to elaborate, from simple to complex-and-batteries-required. One person's favorite is another person's torture. Keep your child's personality in mind when choosing a potty seat or potty chair. Better yet, let him be involved in the selection. A razzle-dazzle child might love bells and whistles and music when he pees. Another child might prefer to decorate his own potty chair and let his own imagination transform his chair into a potty throne.

Either way, introduce your child to his potty chair or seat by explaining this is where he will pee and poop one day. He already knows that he has a high chair or booster seat for eating, and maybe a small table and chair for playing. The next step is learning he has a place to potty, just like mommy and daddy have a special place to potty. The intellectual and emotional connections are made through ongoing familiarity with his potty place.

Your child gets acquainted with his potty chair in three basic steps. The first is ownership, in which he learns, "Look, this is mine!" "Mine" is a powerful word for your toddler. Let him revel in the feeling, especially when something really is his. Talk about the potty chair as his potty and the big toilet as your potty. Say, "Look, we both have potty places. One is big and one is little—just like us!"

The next step is appropriate use, in which he learns what to do with this new chair or seat. He can sit on the potty chair; he can read on his potty chair; he can play with a doll on his potty chair. He may not use his potty chair to climb onto the bathroom counter. He may not throw small toys into the potty chair. He may not use his potty chair instead of a chair at the dinner table. The same with the potty seat. It fits on the toilet "just right." It's not a hat or a Frisbee. It's to use when you want to use the potty.

The last step is *making friends* with his potty, when he decides "Yes, I like this." Your child is interested in using the potty chair and spending time there learning about what his body can do. When he reaches this step, he is not frightened, intimidated, or overwhelmed by the existence of his potty chair.

> Update child-proofing in the potty training bathroom for your child's new skill levels. If you haven't thought about child-proofing since your child was a baby, you may have overlooked the medicine chest and high shelves that are now easier for him to reach. You may also have to remove toilet locks and put the toilet paper back on the roller.

Cleaning the Potty Chair

Taking responsibility for the potty chair is a continuation of your child taking responsibility for his body. Follow your child's interest here. If he wants to help empty the potty, he will be learning valuable self-sufficiency skills that will make your life easier in the long run. Your child probably won't see his helpful efforts as causing more work for you. So try not to worry about perfection—accept any approximation of careful assistance.

You should, however, discourage recklessness. Potty training and bathrooms are supposed to be fun, but they are not a free-for-all. You may need to slow down overly zealous helpers. Remind them that splashing the pee makes more to clean-up. If you sense your child is playing more than helping, thank him for his effort and give him something else to do.

Children evolve into competent helpers through routines and experience. Coercion only leads to conflict. As mentioned earlier, there is no room for conflict in successful potty training. If your child is not a willing helper, wait until after potty training to add this extra skill.

Potty Training Foods

Last but not least, the right potty training foods will also add to a positive potty training environment. Obviously, eating and pottying go hand-in-hand. Potty training is easier if you are giving your child plenty of fluids and nonbinding foods. High-fiber foods keep things moving. Too much dairy slows things down.

Give your child healthy meals and snacks. Brown rice, wheat and multigrain breads, bran cereals and muffins, fresh and dried fruits, and fresh vegetables all help digestion. Prune juice, peach nectar, and pear nectar ease constipation. Also give plenty of water. Limit junk foods, high-fat foods, and dairy. Avoid giving him crackers, cookies, and sweets that fill him up before he eats the healthy high-fiber foods. Reduce white flour breads and pastas. Monitor daily amounts of dairy products with milk and cheese. Also, decrease portions of bananas and apple sauce if he is complaining of hard poops or seems to be pushing too hard.

Great teachers know that a well designed environment is like having an extra teacher by your side. Congratulations! You have now all the essentials for a positive potty environment, which means you have extra help and support for your potty training adventure. You have taken a giant step toward a successful potty experience with a home that fits your child's potty needs in both size and style.

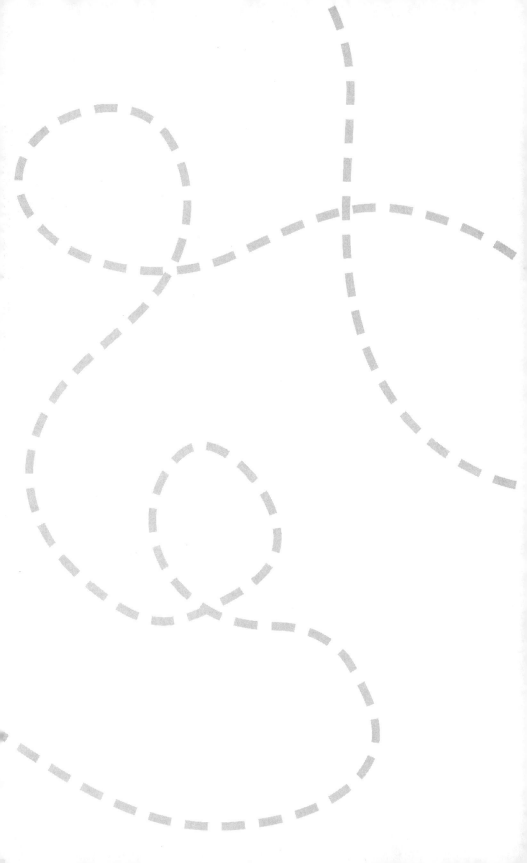

5

Playful Potty Partners

Most children do not potty train themselves. Your child welcomes guidance and support from you. Even when all the readiness factors are in place, you still have an important job to do:

- You describe.
- You explain.
- You answer questions, spoken and unspoken.
- You teach problem solving.
- You generalize skills to new contexts and explain again.
- You teach how to handle change, set backs, and mistakes.
- You become a measure of successes, large and small.
- You give love and make everything worthwhile.

In the wonderful spirit of play, you make potty training less threatening, less scary, and less overwhelming. You make it fun because you are celebrating your child's discoveries about her body and every possible potty situation. You set the perfect potty example as your child grows into her new potty skills.

Becoming a Playful Potty Role Model

Now, more than ever, your child is watching you. She is studying what you do and what you say, and especially what you *don't* say. Watch out, she's probably taking notes too! Consider the following:

- Are you open or secretive about your bathroom behavior?
- Are you following a potty hygiene routine?
- Do you believe your child will be successful in her own time?
- Is potty training a genuine priority or do you fit it in when it's convenient for you?
- Do you talk about your child's potty abilities to other adults in front of your child?
- Do you talk about dirty diapers or soiled clothes as "icky," "yucky," or "nasty?"
- Can you see potty training through your child's eyes to prevent your own boredom and burn-out?

Be aware of unconscious potty messages you might be giving your child. As a positive potty role model, you want her to see you using the potty and not see you taking any bathroom shortcuts that you wouldn't want her to take, such as not washing your hands. You want your actions *and* your words to reflect the same positive potty message. Remember, children learn from what you do more than from what you say. Mixed messages—dreading potty times, rushing through potty times because of other commitments, expressing frustration to adults—will sabotage your positive efforts.

Potty Training Language

As the potty role model, you will also choose the words to use for potty training. There are many choices but only a few that you will feel comfortable using on a daily basis. Choose words that seem natural to you. But avoid overly cute words or words from other languages that will not be recognized by other family members and caregivers. Your child needs to communicate her potty needs to many people, including teachers.

The recommendation for body parts is more specific. Try to use proper names for body parts: penis and vagina. Your child needs to know the proper names even if you use other cute or affectionate terms as well. At this age, your child is learning to identify numerous body parts, not just these. Get started with the right vocabulary now and avoid creating shame or confusion down the road.

You may hear yourself saying, "That's private," to your child when she doesn't really understand what that

> **Potty training is personal. You are learning about how your child learns and masters her body and her world. You are learning about yourself as a teacher—what frustrates you and what inspires you. Your child's potty training experiences involve trust, decision making, perseverance through mistakes, and the ability to conquer obstacles.**

means. Privacy is a difficult concept for young children. Socially appropriate boundaries around pottying are ambiguous and probably better left for a time after your child has mastered the potty process. Questions during the potty training process need to be answered immediately regardless of the potential embarrassment of the adults present. In most cases, a direct public explanation of "We're potty training" should excuse any violations of etiquette.

This is a time, however, to label parts of your child's body (i.e., penis and vagina) as private. That applies to all the body parts covered by a bathing suit. Potty training is the first step in a multi-year process of teaching your child that she owns her body. For better or for worse, she decides what she likes and what she doesn't like. You want your child to believe the power of her own voice, even when she says "You can't make me."

By thinking about your potty training language, you insure that your words and actions consistently express the same positive potty message to your little learner. Candid potty language establishes a secure relationship between your child and her body. The right words build that essential foundation of trust and openness.

Words of Encouragement

The right words to encourage potty success are equally important as your potty language. Two common phrases, "big boy" and "big girl" have the potential to create a negative reaction in some children. Under ideal circumstances, your child hears the phrase as a positive description of growing up. In reality, these phrases can backfire on you. If there's a younger sibling in the house who is a sweet attention-magnet, being "little" is better than being "big." Your "big" boy might opt for a high stakes negative alternative like deliberating peeing on the Oriental rug.

Focus on *body smart* instead. What does "big" really mean? It means smart, clever, strong, capable, quick, thoughtful, and so on. Talking about "body smart" connects the new skills to your child's body—exactly where you want his attention to be.

When it comes to vocabulary and behavior, your child learns more about potty priorities from watching you than from a perfect potty script. Remember that your child's learning, and potty training in particular, is personal. Your child is not just learning facts and skills. She's learning from you, about you, in order to become someone.

Language and Imagination

You may have noticed that your child talks about her favorite TV and video characters as if they lived next door. To her, these are not merely fictional characters. They are friends who can be very powerful potty training partners. They can share your child's potty journey, motivate her to try new things, as well as console and celebrate through setbacks and successes. See Chapter Nine for more information on how to incorporate these characters in your child's positive potty routine.

The potty training role model immerses the new potty-goer in the wonderful world of potties. You set the example that potty going is fun and easy. You create rich new language experiences that ease the child into new ways of thinking about her body. You invite your child to step into unknown territory with old friends and new friends eager to share in this journey. Take full advantage of your child's emerging language skills. Find words and phrases that convey clear, reassuring messages about your child's upcoming potty adventure.

Happy Potty Helpers

Approach potty training as a team effort. Your child's personal potty team includes the primary potty training partner, the potty training assistants (anyone who will be speaking to your child about her potty adventures), potty cheerleaders, and finally your parent-support allies. You want to include the entire team in your playful potty training strategies.

The Primary Partner

Some households may have the luxury of multiple candidates for the primary potty training position: stay-at-home parents, work-at-home parents, live-in grandparents or full-time nannies. Choose the person who has the time and the emotional compatibility with your particular child. This person has the responsibility for orchestrating the potty play days that will be discussed in the following chapter.

The Assistants

The assistants on the team can be co-parents, siblings, and anyone else taking your child to the potty. Let your assistants know your child's favorite potty songs and games. They might feel a little self-conscious singing or playing them at first, but they might discover they're having fun too. The primary potty partner is free to ask these helpful assistants to jump in when he or she is unavailable and to help out in any way, as long as they agree to act consistently with the positive potty adventure.

Siblings as Helpers

Siblings are a huge asset to the social aspect of potty training. Little ones learn by example. The more they are immersed in a world of potty-going people, the more they internalize the implicit expectation that this is how it should be done. Then it's just a matter of time until they discover that their body works the same way.

Older siblings also provide important motivation. What child doesn't want to be just like a respected older sibling? Young children are watching the people they love with fearless devotion. That desire will expedite potty learning once the physical control is in place.

But you don't have to go out and borrow an older child during the potty training months. Young children have the uncanny ability to recruit all kinds of interesting people into their potty training world.

The Cheerleaders

Every positive learning adventure needs cheerleaders. Rally anyone and everyone to non-coercively support and encourage your child. Cheerleaders share your child's successes and stay positive in the face of setbacks and challenges. Cheerleaders know and believe that she will be a successful potty-goer in good time and are always there to inspire a forward looking attitude.

Parent-Support Allies

Potty training can be challenging, so the team ought to include cheerleaders for the parents, too. These can be phone friends who will lend a sympathetic ear during problematic times, experienced parents who will remind you that your child is normal, and pinch hitters you can call on when you have a schedule conflict. Important parenting challenges should not be handled alone.

Working with Your Potty Team

Good communication brings your team together. First build consensus among everyone living in your home. You will invest considerable time and energy in formulating an individualized potty plan for your child. You've had time to think about your child's individual personality and her personal potty training strengths, but this discussion may be the first time the others have given any thought to the subject of potty training. However, they probably have a few assumptions and expectations from their own experiences. Do not rush into potty training until everyone is on the same page.

Brief everyone, including the extended team. Talk to grandparents and all your potty helpers. Explain your playful potty training goals. Tell them how you'd like them to help. Be specific. If they are receptive, share encouraging phrases and the fun parts of your potty routine. They want to be successful, not frustrated.

Everyone wants what is best for your child—to be successful, to grow in a timely way, and to avoid the physical and mental stress of a negative experience. Reassure everyone that rushing only delays progress. You are the person who knows your child best. Give others your time-proven tips to best support your child.

Happy Home and School Connections

Your potty team also includes your child's teachers and caregivers. Pottying at school may be different from pottying at home—different bathrooms, different fixtures, different routines, and different people. Communication is the key to managing these differences. You want to know as much as possible about the potty routine at school.

Preschools set policies about potty training according to each school's educational philosophy. You should discuss any concerns about your child's potty readiness prior to enrolling her. Most schools understand firsthand the process and problems associated with potty training. These schools will be able to evaluate an appropriate starting date for your child and possibly even assist you in your efforts.

Think of school as your ally, not as an antagonist. Early childhood programs share in your child's care and education, and are an important partner in your child's early years. If possible, begin a new school relationship with an attitude of mutual decision making and trust.

Sometimes the school experience helps children with the final steps of potty training, as children learn from their pottying peers. For example, daily routines include potty breaks that add a predictable structure to potty choices. Lastly, the classroom teacher is often a neutral adult that your child is eager to please.

Questions to ask about the potty routine at school:
- What time do the children potty?
- Do the children go potty as a group or individually?
- Is the teacher near the children or at the door?
- How does the teacher talk to the children about successes and mistakes?
- How do the other children talk about successes and mistakes?
- How is your child doing in non-potty related school activities?

Any differences from home can create resistance to pottying at school. Stay positive about the school and about the teachers as you help your child adapt her home skills to this new world away from home.

Be Flexible with the School's Methods

Some schools will adapt to your child's potty needs while others will ask her to adapt to the school routine. Trust and communication are essential either way. Listen to the school's perspective. They usually have professional experience with many children in this situation and hopefully have appropriate developmental expectations for the children in their program. Ask the school to listen to your personal experience as someone who best appreciates your child's strengths and abilities. Try to avoid creating a high stress situation for your child.

- Give your child time if she just started a new school, has a new teacher, or is in a new class. She will master the potty part of her day after she masters the other changes.
- Share your playful home strategies with the teacher to create a familiar experience for your child. For example, the teacher might enjoy singing your child's potty song.
- Build your child's trust in her teacher. She might not understand that her teacher is ready and willing to help. Assure her by saying, for example, "Ms. So-and-so can help you with your pants. Just tell her when you need her . . . and be sure she's listening when you talk." Try role-playing if your child is hesitant.
- Ask the teacher if your child can potty last if she is overwhelmed by a group of children in the bathroom. Or ask if your child can be taken solo.
- Design encouraging notes that can be put in your child's lunchbox or delivered by the teacher at potty time. Make them reader-friendly by copying some home/school potty pictures or just a big "I love you" heart.
- Give potty reports back and forth from school to home. Keep it light ("just checking"). Let your child see that you and the teacher are working together in a positive way.

Your attitude toward school policies and school personalities directly affects your child's ability to thrive away from home. Try to establish an effective, working partnership.

Peer Pressure

Potty-age children are part of an ever-growing social world that includes both school and neighborhood. This awareness of other children and other children's abilities opens the door to positive peer influences on your child's potty behavior, particularly after three years of age. Peers often add a new motivation for potty training but only if adults are not adding negative competition to the child's experience. Negative comparisons have a potential for escalating into a power struggle. For example, your child could respond, "Oh yeah . . . you say look at her. Look at me; I can make your life miserable!" Like natural consequences, let the peer experience do the teaching without emotionally charged lectures comparing children's abilities.

Stick to simple, emotionally neutral descriptions when talking about peer behavior. If you invite a potty trained friend to your home during potty play times, let the potty trained child lead the potty experience. Be the "invisible hand" creating opportunities for interest. If your child isn't already curious about her friend's behavior, you won't inspire interest.

Similarly, when your child is at preschool, your prompting may cause resistance. Stand back. Allow your child to observe and choose. Should your child express a desire to "kick the diapers" or show concern that she's the last one wearing diapers, tell her clearly that you are ready to help her. And get ready for playful potty training.

Dealing with Criticism

Everyone doesn't always agree with your parenting choices. So everyone won't always agree with playful potty training. Some people will tell you that you can potty train in a day. Your mother might remember that you were potty trained at nine months. Your best friend may think your child just needs a good push. Regrettably, you might never change their minds. Continue to be your child's number one advocate with gracefulness, knowing that stress and potty training do not mix. Here's a chance to extend your positive playful attitude to adults.

When talking to adults, keep the focus on what's best for your child. State your goals for positive potty training in advance. Explain your confidence in your child's ability to potty train in good time. Remind people that it's okay to respectfully disagree. Try to stay calm knowing that everything sounds more personal when it's about your child. Sometimes it's simply best to take a "potty training break" from people who want to embarrass or push your child into uncomfortable situations.

Most importantly, be a positive role model for your child. Use your best problem solving strategies to describe the other person's point of view to your child without critical harshness. So when grandma comes to the house with a bagful of candy to entice your child to use the potty, simply explain to your child that grandma thinks that's fun but you still want her to use the potty just because she needs to. Remind your child that you are her potty partner. If someone says something directly to your child that feels hurtful—like asking her "When are you going to grow up and use the potty like a big girl?"—be ready with a hug. Explain that the two of you are learning together and will solve all problems together. You will be teaching your child the bigger lesson of how to maneuver in a world where people disagree.

What if Mom and Dad Disagree?

Your playful potty attitude is critical to success with all your potty partners but especially with a spouse who will be seeing, hearing, and possibly also handling daily potty-times. It's inevitable that two grown people with two different personal histories and possibly two different temperament styles will sometimes disagree. Your playful potty attitude is here to remind you to be flexible and focus on a positive experience for your child.

Remember that minor differences in potty training will prepare your child to be adaptable to different personalities and situations in the world.

Cultivate your relaxed, playful attitude when disagreements begin to feel stressful. Try the following:

- Imagine this is a sitcom—Odd Couple stories are funny if you can step back a little
- Stretch a little—take a baby step out of what feels like the "only way"
- Refuel your optimism—your child will be potty trained one day
- Take a silliness break—all stress undermines potty training

The positive potty environment definitely includes the grown-ups in your child's world. Therefore, part of successful potty training includes managing disagreements without getting sidetracked.

Sometimes, no matter how hard Mom and Dad try to be consistent potty partners, both parents do not agree. Hopefully you tried. Hopefully your positive, playful attitude has prevented you from criticizing one another. But if you tried everything and must agree to disagree, here are a few important parenting guidelines to help maintain an atmosphere of mutual respect. These strategies also apply to parents and grandparents, parents and teachers, and anyone who shares responsibility for raising a child.

- Whoever is interacting with the child at the time of the disagreement is in charge of the situation. If one parent is playing potty games when the other parent thinks the child should be in bed, the parent in charge is the one who started the interaction with the child. It doesn't matter at this moment who is right or wrong. What matters is that one parent doesn't criticize the other parent in front of the child. The parent-in-charge gets to finish whatever was started. The other parent is free to go for a walk or put on earphones.

- Talk about potty training disagreements *after* the incident in question has passed and when your child is away or sleeping. It's always easier to talk about disagreements after emotions have cooled down. Wait until you can speak calmly to continue. Focus on the potty training goal and your child's short-term successes. Make modifications because they work for your child, not necessarily because they work for the adults.
- Children learn different rules for different situations. As long as you are consistent with yourself, your child will know what each of you expects and how to manage those expectations. Simply explain the differences to your child; for example, "When you go to the store with daddy, you have to follow daddy's rules."
- Your child will learn how to adapt to different people in the real world. And she won't play one parent against the other. Now, you've turned a parenting negative into a parenting positive.

Positive, Playful, and Prepared

Potty training has a reputation for being difficult because sometimes parents overlook all of the factors that influence the potty training experience. You, on the other hand, are prepared! Your playful preparation will ease you into active potty training with the best possible attitude and environment for success. Most importantly, your playful spirit will enable you to face the unexpected with resourcefulness and humor.

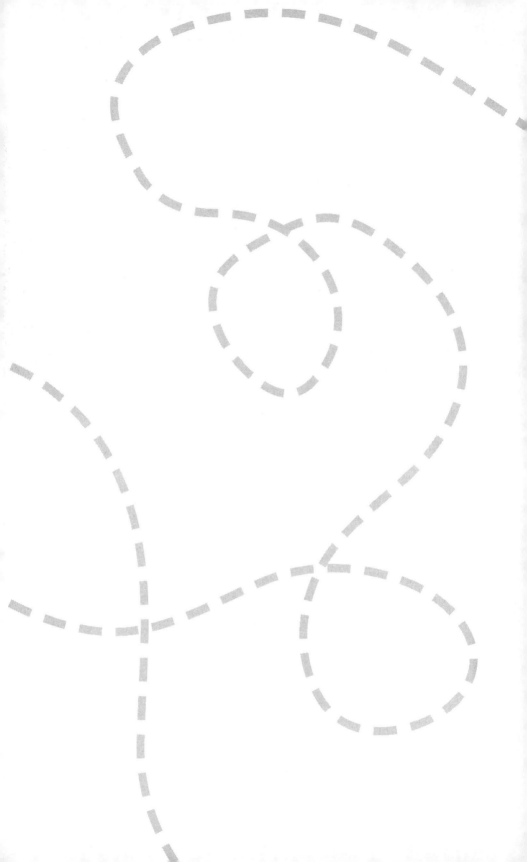

Part Two

Active Potty Training

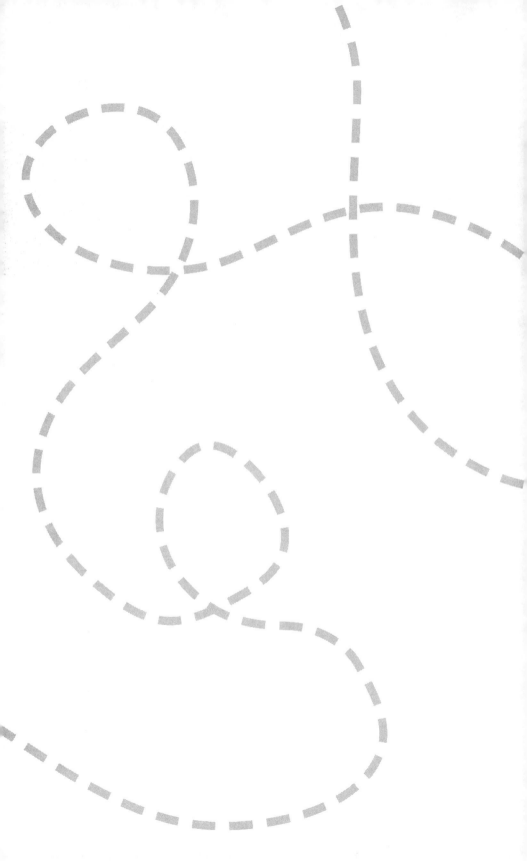

Potty Play Days

Your child is now ready. He understands how his body works. He has the physical ability to control his body. He is interested and willing to learn new daily routines.

You are ready. You have the time and the energy to teach a new potty routine. You've been talking about potty training with your child. You've created a positive potty environment at home. It's time to start active potty training.

Potty Play Days are designated times that you help your child practice potty training in a supportive playful setting. Clear your schedule and your child's schedule for the weekend or for a block of hours when he can take off his diaper (clothes are optional) and practice his newly emerging potty skills. Some children have practiced potty training "in their heads" so many times they master potty training on the first potty play day. Others are so eager, they will learn anything to avoid putting that diaper back on again. Parents are happily relieved in those two scenarios. If you are not a parent of one of these instant potty-goers, that's okay.

Know your child. Most children need time to learn new routines. Most children need time to feel confident. Most children learn through trial and error. So while some potty play days will last a day or a weekend, most will last a week or two. Potty play days are opportunities to explore and test potty skills under optimal conditions, when you and your child are less distracted by other day-to-day obligations.

This chapter presents three variations of potty play days for your child's optimal success: a one-time potty weekend, a series of potty practice afternoons, and weekend mini-sessions. By customizing your potty plan, you will find the perfect match for you and your child.

You can make an educated guess about whether your child is a weekend potty learner or an extended-days potty-learner based on how he approaches change and new situations. If your child jumps into new experiences quickly and easily, he may master potty training in one weekend (if all the readiness factors are in place). If your child approaches new situations cautiously and tentatively, he may prefer the slow-and-steady potty course with multiple potty play days, and possibly even a week or two to build enough confidence to finally let go of the security of diaper wearing. If you aren't sure, watch your child's reaction to the first potty play days. How's he doing? Is he having frequent potty success? If not, where does he seem to run into difficulty? Difficulty is not a negative. It's the place you find your cues as to the kind of support to give your child.

> **During potty training, your child may face disappointment, confusion, mistakes, and fears. Temperament, timing, environment, and routines are all precedents for how your child learns to handle age-appropriate dilemmas. If your child is intrigued by the potty process, the thrill of mastery will overshadow the obstacles along the way.**

Getting Started

Let your child know in advance when potty play days are coming. Depending on his temperament, you can tell him a week before or the day before. Some children need a longer time to get ready for a new experience while others might fret if given too much time to anticipate a changing routine.

You can judge your child's needs by considering how he would anticipate an exciting upcoming event, like a vacation to Disney World. If telling him a long time in advance would make him happy and have him dancing around the house excited about sleeping in a hotel and talking to Snow White, advance warning is really positive planning. If telling him in advance would make him a little anxious about who will feed the fish while you're away, then wait until the day before to give him a sneak preview but not too much information. Everything in potty training can be custom-fit.

What You'll Need

Potty training is easier if you have everything you need ready in the place when you need it. If you have what you need, you are also prepared to teach the new routine the first time you do it, which is especially important for those parents and children who thrive on consistency.

- Stock your kitchen with potty-friendly drinks and snacks.
- Gather a basket of children's potty books.
- Buy your choice of fun-to-wear pull-ups or training pants.
- Select outfits that include easy on/easy off clothing (no overalls, tight clothes, hard-to-undo buttons or special care clothes).
- Choose your potty chair or potty seat (with themes, colors, or styles that appeal to your child).
- Find a stepstool for easy hand washing.

- Add some new themed hand towels or fun soap to the potty bathroom (optional).
- Choose your cleanup product for accidents (extra towels, floor cleaner, disinfectant).
- Pick a place for wet or soiled laundry, preferably a place your child can throw his own clothes as needed.

Basic Structure

The basic structure of potty play days is the same whether you choose to potty train for one weekend or a few hours at a time on multiple days. It has a playful name that distinguishes it from other activities and clearly communicates the goal of potty-going. Most of all, potty play days are positive and celebrate the small successes that lead to the big successes.

A designated potty play time reminds you not to schedule too many other things. As a result, your child perceives this time as casual fun with you, with the personalized attention as an added bonus. Keep your potty expectations clear and simple by choosing a few key phrases that your child can repeat as often as needed. For example, "Tomorrow will be fun! We'll play and potty at home all weekend."

Start your potty play time with a ritual. Ring a potty time kick-off bell or sing an "it's potty time" song. Then take off any stay-dry,

> Your potty-age child is most likely in a developmental stage of wanting to know what's coming next. Remember, emotional comfort and intellectual predictability go hand-in-hand. Or as the adults say, "knowledge is power." While you may be ready to begin tomorrow, your child probably needs a little more advance warning.

feel-dry diapers. For the next few hours, stay attentive, playing and doing simple chores while waiting and watching for potty opportunities. Given that your child is already staying dry longer, his potty breaks may be every hour or hour and a half. Now, off to the bathroom.

Bathroom Routines

Routines have amazing teaching power. One of the developmental characteristics of potty training-aged-children is a love of sequence and order. Each time you visit the bathroom on potty play days, your child will practice the same potty sequence. First we potty; then we wipe and flush; and then we wash and sing. Your child will feel competent and capable—"hooray, look at what I can do!" The predictable, repetitive sequence gives him a sense of order that is easy to master. Use this cognitive awareness to take the stress out of sometimes confusing potty choices. Here are some fun ways to build a positive potty routine:

- Show your child how much toilet paper is "just enough." Pulling toilet paper can be a game of counting squares or measuring lengths.
- Show your child how to properly wipe after pottying—front to back, front to back. Add some silliness when you ask your child, "Wait, which way do we wipe? Back to front? No, no, no. It's front to back."
- Introduce "fearless flushing." Try to prepare your child for that unexpected noisy, splashing toilet by making flushing a magic act. Give him control by counting off, "three, two, and one, flush!" Or, close the lid and wave abracadabra, and open to see if everything disappeared.
- Teach your child how to be a "conservationist" (there's a fun word for your child to repeat). Have a one-time flush rule. And only flush when there's something in the toilet.

- If you're using a potty chair, use the same routine each time to empty the potty and flush. Children enjoy playing "what do we do next?" and the sequence gives them a sense of ownership and control.
- Conclude your bathroom fun with happy hand-washing. Your child needs a concrete reminder to wash hands for a sufficient length of time to be hygienic. A song is the perfect reminder. Try "Happy Potty to Me":

  Happy potty to me.
  Happy potty to me.
  I'm learning where to pee.
  Happy potty to me.
  Happy potty to me.
  Happy potty to me.
  I'm learning where to pooopie.
  Happy potty to me.

- Your child might also enjoy fun foam or character soap in his favorite potty bathroom. Even when potty attempts are futile, you are still reinforcing good hygienic behavior.

The Potty-Body Connection

Some children learn to pee on the potty first while others learn to poop on the potty first. As your child learns to read the physical sensations of his body, he has more control over where to potty. He may know with more certainty that a poop is coming and therefore be more likely to get to the potty in time. Or he may feel a poop coming and prefer to poop in the diaper because the diaper is more familiar. One child may feel the need to pee, stop everything, and enjoy getting to the potty on time while his twin brother might feel the need to pee, try to hold it until he finishes what he's doing, and rarely make it to the potty in time. Each child is different.

In all cases, try to approach potty training the same way—by teaching the same general principles and creating realistic potty routines. Success will usually come in small steps. Some children will pee on the potty before they poop on the potty. Others will poop on the potty before they pee on the potty. Either way, build from your child's initial place of comfort.

If your child poops at regular times, incorporate potty time for pooping into your daily routine. This will help him make the potty–poop connection. If your child has both an interest and the physical ability to wait to poop until he gets to the potty, he may prefer to poop on the potty on a regular basis.

The choice is completely up to your child. Once your child learns he can control the sphincter muscles, he has the power to exert that control at will. He can also choose not to poop, either in opposition to external demands or in a desire to maintain a sense of security. Always respect your child's choice if he chooses not to poop on the potty.

In regards to both peeing and pooping, help your child identify the physical sensations by saying aloud in a simple, descriptive way, "Look, I think your body is saying it's ready to pee or poop." Then use potty play days to help your child be successful when he chooses the potty option. Help him get to the bathroom on time, relax enough to "let go," and see the success of going pee and poop on the potty.

Wiping

Shortcuts to proper wiping turn into poor hygiene habits. For girls, wiping away from the vagina will help prevent urinary tract infections. It may take years for your child to perfect thorough wiping, but you can always be a good role model. When you start potty practice, as well as any time you are handling toilet paper, take the opportunity to mention the right way to wipe. Ask your child to show you how she wipes herself. Gently remind her to "clean front to back" and accept all approximations, even if you find her "wiping" her tummy instead. Some children may wipe from the back between their legs. Others wipe from in front of their legs. Some are contortionists. Others are dainty. Many different methods work, as long as the job gets done.

Potty Training Boys

If you are the parent of a boy, you have the additional decision of whether to teach your son to pee standing up or sitting down. It's best to keep it simple at first. In the beginning, teach your son to sit to pee and to poop. Once he understands the logistics, he will want to imitate his male role models. When your son is motivated to imitate his stand-up male role models, you can get him a stepstool to reach the adult-size toilet.

It is usually helpful for boys to practice peeing and pooping while sitting on the potty, rather than trying to learn sitting and standing at the same time. Once your son understands the logistics of peeing into the potty, he can then learn to imitate his stand-up male role models.

Same-gender role models can make learning easier. Your child won't need to make any logical inferences about what's the same and what's different if he sees similar anatomy, whether he sees daddy, older siblings, or male classmates at school. Not to worry, though; there's no evidence that female potty teachers significantly inhibit a boy's potty learning.

Practice Makes Perfect

Athletes and musicians know that repetition is essential to mastery. Each time your child uses the potty, he integrates something new into the total potty experience: "I understand signals from my body" or "I wasn't ready this time"; "A big splash surprised me" or "it didn't surprise me at all"; "I like running to the potty because I feel smart and in control" or "I don't like these interruptions at all." All of these discoveries transform a potty novelty into something ordinary and predictable. This is when potty practice becomes potty habit.

Your child also encounters the new potty expectation that using the potty is a priority. Initially, you are the time-management expert as you take your child for potty breaks every few hours using a positive potty reminder. Eventually, your child shares your goal of getting to the potty every time. Success begins to feel like something normal.

Types of Potty Play Days

Here are three types of potty play days that you can adapt to your specific needs: the Potty Weekend, Naked Noons and Weekend Minis. The Potty Weekend works best for parents who like structure and for children who adapt more quickly to change. Naked Noons work best for parents who can maintain consistency for an extended time and for children who like a slow and steady pace. Weekend Minis are for those households where weekday schedules do not allow for consistent afternoon sessions and one potty weekend is not enough.

Potty Weekends

Choosing a Potty Weekend says that you and your child are ready to make the leap into the world of underwear. You believe your child wants to take charge of his body and his environment. This weekend gives him the opportunity to practice potty-going under ideal circumstances with your support and encouragement.

- Name the event. This reinforces the intention of the weekend. For example, you might say, "Tomorrow is our Potty Weekend!"

- Tell your child the goal. "We'll play and potty at home all weekend. Then you can say bye-bye to your diapers."
- Practice the goal under the simplest conditions. Your plan for the weekend is all about making pottying simple and easy for your child. Take off the diapers so your child can feel his body working. Dress him in easy-off clothing or no clothes at all. He will then have immediate feedback as to what happens without a diaper and an easier time getting on the potty in a timely way.
- Teach potty hygiene. Bathrooms are very fun places, but the boundaries are sometimes not obvious. Start with clear messages about how to use the toilet paper, how many times to flush the toilet, and a fun hand-washing habit. Sing the "Happy Potty" song (see page 68) to teach your child how long hand washing should take.
- Practice makes perfect. A Potty Weekend gives your child two days of concentrated potty practice. You are an active partner, thinking for two until your child assumes greater responsibility for planning those well-timed potty breaks. Each visit to the potty builds confidence and understanding for the next potty experience.
- A happy ending. No matter what happens on this weekend, you've hopefully had a very personal, fun-filled time with your child. Tell your child how much you enjoyed being with him. If your child is ready, gift wrap those favorite underpants. If your child is still learning, focus on the successes rather than the failures and read ahead to "Weekend Minis" for a Sunday night potty celebration. Either way, you have everything you need to evaluate your child's future potty training behavior.

Naked Noons

Naked Noons is a series of potty practice days for those who find the Potty Weekend too overwhelming. Just like the Potty Weekend, it reminds you to give potty training your relaxed yet deliberate focus.

- Name the time. Since "Naked Noons" is fun to say, it also must be fun to do. Your Naked Noons are a meaningful part of the daily routine, just like daily story-time.
- Tell your child the goal. "Naked Noons is our time every day to play and potty at home. Then you can say bye-bye to your diapers."
- Practice the goal under the simplest conditions. Begin the Naked Noon with your starting ritual. It's time to take off your child's clothes or change him out of his diaper and into pull-ups. For the next three to four hours, you will be busy playing and doing simple chores while always waiting and watching for potty opportunities. Given that your child is already staying dry longer, your potty breaks will be every hour or hour and a half.
- Teach potty hygiene. Even when potty attempts are futile, you are still reinforcing great bathroom behavior. This insures that bathrooms are fun, happy places that your child wants to visit.
- Practice makes perfect. Schedule Naked Noons for a span of two weeks. It's better to include weekend afternoons in your plan, if possible. If not, assume you may need a third week. You will have a good idea of your child's improvement over that period of time and how much longer, if any, you need to proceed.
- A happy ending. You don't want to be held hostage to your Naked Noons. Their effectiveness ends when you or your child is wishing to be anywhere else but there. Plan for a realistic "happy ending." At the end of the first week, acknowledge some achievement by your child. You may not be shopping for underpants if your child isn't ready, but you can buy some fun new hand towels or character soaps, or make a photo book with pictures from the week, called "My Naked Noons."

Weekend Minis

In some households, you cannot commit to an entire day of potty training or to a week of potty afternoons. If that's the case, you can plan one month of mini-sessions on Saturdays and Sundays, for two to three hours in the morning or in the afternoon. Pick the time of day that matches your child's best mood. If your child hits the day running, choose mornings. If your child sleeps late and hits his stride after lunch, choose afternoons.

- Name the time. You can still use Naked Noons or Potty Play Days.

- Tell your child the goal. "This weekend we'll have Potty Play Days to play and potty at home. Then, in a few weeks, you can say bye-bye to your diapers."

- Practice the goal under the simplest conditions. Start your potty play times with a starting ritual and take off those diapers. Designate a time span that will give your child adequate practice. You will want to "watch and wait" for at least two to three potty opportunities each potty play day.

- Teach potty hygiene. Continue with fun bathroom rituals— using "just enough" toilet paper, the proper way to wipe, fearless flushing, and of course washing hands to the "Happy Potty" song. Your child is learning through repetition. Each happy bathroom-time reinforces a positive goal.

- Practice makes perfect. Schedule potty play days for four consecutive weekends. Because there are five off-days in between your potty play days, weekend minis seem to take longer but it really isn't much practice time. These are relaxed times when your child is learning how his body works. Do not continue if your child is not making some connection between taking off his diapers and the choice to pee on the potty. But if your child asks, allow him to go without diapers during the week in controlled settings.

- A happy ending. Potty play days are supposed to be a fun time spent together. Plan to acknowledge your child's achievement at the end of each weekend. Were you counting all the times he peed and pooped on the toilet? After Sunday night dinner, present a "Happy Potty" cake with candles for each time your child used the potty. Save the burnt candles. The cake will shine brighter and brighter each week and you can have fun counting all the candles at the end of the month.

Your Personal Potty Plan

Your personal potty plan takes into account all the potty and personality factors that could possibly undermine your success. Consider your child's natural temperament, your current lifestyle, as well as any mediating factors like holidays or upcoming vacations that might disrupt your routines. Use the following guide to see which plan best fits your child and your family at this particular time.

Potty Weekend	Naked Noons	Weekend Mini's Potty Play Days
More structured	More structured	Less Structured
Depends on previous activities	High consistency	Low consistency
More adaptability required	Low adaptability required	High adaptability required
Faster pace	Gradual pace	Gradual pace
Intense focus	Gentle focus	Gentle focus
More potential for independence	More potential for cooperation	More potential for independence
High frustration potential	Low frustration potential	More frustration potential

Are you still unsure of which plan is just right for you? Here are a few others factors you can consider.

Are You an Unstructured Parent?

Unstructured parents can feel too confined by a single Potty Weekend. They can unknowingly sabotage the consistent routine of Potty Weekends by not sticking to the basic structure.

Sometimes this lack of structure makes it more difficult to give children clear expectations and support. If you're an unstructured parent, you should:

- Solicit the help of someone who can keep you on task; for example, a telephone friend who will call every few hours throughout the weekend.
- Recruit another family member to be a hands-on substitute or teaching partner.
- Try regular mini-sessions like Naked Noons, when you can commit to a few hours of a simplified potty routine.

Are You a Weekend Warrior?

The weekend warrior lifestyle may be too intense for a single Potty Weekend. The child who was not gently introduced to the potty plan during the week can easily become overwhelmed. Weekend warriors should:

- Double-check their preliminary efforts during the two weeks before the Potty Weekend. Remember, potty training is a long distance marathon that requires warm-up time; it's not a cold sprint.
- Relax. Begin the Potty Weekend and each individual day with a calming affirmation—"I teach with love and kindness."
- Include preplanned fun activities to balance the tendency to be consumed by a potty agenda. Open-ended activities such as blocks, trucks, new dancing songs, and games work best for long days at home.

Are You a Busy Parent?

Life is busy. There are times in your life when you must juggle more than a sane number of balls in the air. The potty training months may coincide with a critical project at work. Your mother-in-law could be recuperating in your house from a hospital procedure. Here are some suggestions that can help you integrate potty training into a busy schedule:

- Try to integrate mini-sessions with other child care routines.
- Solicit a realistic time management buddy to review your plans before you begin a Potty Weekend.
- Inform friends and family that you are focused on your child at this time, in order to minimize distractions.
- Accept that there will never be a perfect time and do it anyway.
- In all cases, you can substitute afternoon or weekend mini-sessions for a one-time potty weekend.

Do You Have Multiple Children?

You may have too many other family obligations to devote one weekend to a single child. Older siblings may have karate and ballet on opposite sides of town. You're coaching the Sunday afternoon game. Don't forget the pancake breakfast and religious services. Full-house families must either use advance planning or substitute more realistic mini-alternatives.

- Give everyone in the family a part in the potty plan. Create a potty training team with designated fun assignments for older and even younger siblings.
- Preplan. Send siblings to sleep-aways at friends or relatives.
- Consider the afternoon mini-sessions or try multiple weekend mini-sessions.

Tips for Different Temperaments

Easy Temperament

The child with the easy temperament can most likely adapt to any of the potty plans. But in his typical agreeable fashion, he may not care about dirty diapers or potty accidents.

- Clearly communicate the goal of potty play days: To stop what you're doing when you need to use the potty and to say goodbye to diapers.

- Accept that your child might not be bothered by accidents and make sure you have a guilt-free easy cleanup plan, without shame or blame.
- Try not to be too smug in front of your friends about how easy it is to potty train

Slow-to-Warm-Up Temperament

Children with a slow-to-warm-up temperament need time to adapt to change. You can give your slow-to-warm-up child time in a few different ways:

- Extend the length of potty preparation time. Your slow-to-warm-up child wants to practice his potty skills a little at a time and over a long period of time. He prefers mastery in small, manageable pieces rather than in big bites. Stretch his competence slowly by adding new skills and new challenges.
- Use the Potty Weekend as the culmination of months of increasingly successful potty behavior. The slow-to-warm-up child does not like surprises. Hold off on the Potty Weekend until you are confident that mastery is already there for your child. The Potty Weekend then becomes more of a ritual farewell to diapers than a teaching time.
- Naked Noons give a slow-to-warm-up child the opportunity for gradual success with an involved supportive parent. The slow-to-warm-up child also likes the extended daily routine. Anchor the new routine to simple, reassuring messages. For example, "When I go on the potty, I don't need my diaper— hip, hip hooray for me!" Before you know it, you will hear your child repeat those same words to himself as he moves forward through the potty process.
- Weekend Minis are a second option leading to gradual success. The gap in between practice days is manageable for children with strong verbal and cognitive development because they can talk about "what's coming." Slow-to-warm-up children like

to see and talk about the connections between their weekend mini-sessions and their weekday progress. They are not walking over the bridge if they don't believe the beams are strongly anchored to firm ground.

Difficult Temperament

Like the child with a slow-to-warm-up temperament, the child with a difficult temperament does not welcome change. But unlike the child with a slow-to-warm-up temperament, this child is not a receptive partner. He wants it his way and he wants it now.

- Follow your child's lead through the potty preparation process. Give him control over his body and his actions. Creatively add new skills with an invisible hand. Act as if Potty Weekend, Naked Noons or Weekend Minis are his idea.
- Use statements rather than requests for your child's participation. For example, "Time to sit on the potty" rather than "Would you like to sit on the potty?"
- Meltdowns during the Potty Weekend are expected. Be available to comfort or to pick up the pieces and move forward. Refocus on the goal with clear, simple messages. For example, "Sometimes you don't make it to the potty in time. You will next time."
- Each time you begin Naked Noons and Weekend Minis, it requires the problematic task of shifting gears for the child with a difficult temperament. A definitive starting ritual is necessary, as is a strong yet compassionate demeanor from you. You may need to allow your child to fall apart or protest without you questioning the course. Simply wait. He will be ready in time (and his transition time will get shorter each day).
- If you are the parent of a child with a difficult temperament, plan regular rejuvenating breaks for yourself.

Customizing Your Potty Plan

Formally or informally, construct your plan and make it your reference point for the weeks ahead. Personalize the plan with your child's favorite themes and characters. Think of activities that will interest your child at times that are convenient for you. You don't want to be caught at the end of your Potty Weekend without the cupcakes or the right words to encourage your child to the next step.

For those who like the formality of an organizing chart, here is a sample Personal Potty Plan and a blank form to write your own plan.

SIMPLE POTTY PLAN				
We're busy, busy, busy—that's us! But we still like to play. Going on the potty is fun. Let's try it today!				
WHO	**WHAT**	**WHERE**	**WHEN**	**HOW**
Mom Dad Afternoon sitter Date-night sitter Grandparents Neighbors Friend with four-year-old Best friend in Ohio	Snacks, juices, new cereals Princess Pull-Ups Princess potty Princess stool Princess towels Princess hamper Spray bottles Cleaner	Downstairs bath Add potty chair one week before on [date] Remove medicines Take off lock on toilet	Weekend Minis starting June 1—in two weeks Practice Saturday mornings and Sunday after naps Try for one month Ready for party on the fourth of July!	Slow and steady Plan pool time Picnic snacks with princess cups and plates Celebrate Sunday nights with princess cupcakes

OUR PERSONAL POTTY PLAN				
Our Positive Potty Message				
WHO	WHAT	WHERE	WHEN	HOW

Post your plan in a visible place where you will see it daily. Add some positive reminders to reassure you when you feel discouraged, to honor the uniqueness of your child, and to keep you moving positively toward success. These reminders can help get you through a challenging potty day. Remember them when you or your child is frustrated or confused by the potty training process. Keep sight of your long-term goal and revise your short-term goals to be more realistic. Here are some examples:

1. Our Potty Weekend is a chance to growing a little more independent. I will give my child my attention and the tools for successful pottying. Soon, we will say goodbye to diapers— "See ya, don't need ya!"

2. Yeah for our Naked Noons! Take off your diapers and feel how your body works. "I like to practice on the potty—I sit and I try. One day I won't need those bulky diapers to keep me dry!"

3. We're busy, busy, busy—that's us! But we still like to play. Going on the potty is fun. Let's try it today!

4. Hooray for potty days! We eat. We play. We potty. I love my body. Sometimes I like my diaper. Sometimes I like the potty. I always like growing smarter and taller.

Your personal potty plan is a flexible guide to create time and space in your busy day to focus on your child's new potty adventure. It's written with love, not in stone.

When to Take a Break

The purpose of potty play days is to create successful experiences for your child. Do not continue active potty training if your child is not making the connection between taking off the diapers and the choice to pee on the potty. Return to a more casual potty environment until the physical control or emotional desire is more apparent. Potty play days work because your child is ready to choose to use the potty at the right time and because he needs to rehearse thinking and acting on his own. If it isn't "clicking" under these simple circumstances, it will be more frustrating in real life situations. Better to give your child more time.

The Switch to Underwear

Underwear is a big milestone in the potty game. Try not to be too anxious to make the switch. Your child will get his long-awaited underpants after he's demonstrated he can stay dry with ease. If you don't feel fairly confident that the majority of potty training is behind you, don't switch to underwear. You want Las Vegas house odds that your child is mastering the potty routine. He needs the skill and the attitude to say, "See ya, don't need ya!"

After the practice of potty play days, the move to underpants is a *definite goodbye* to diapers—not maybe, not cross your fingers, and not a bribe. Sometimes your child cannot resist the lure of underwear and he'll make promises he can't keep ("Please mommy, please mommy, pleeeeease . . ."). In this instance, you know better than your child if you're setting him up to fail. If the skills are not there, underwear won't make a difference.

There are times when the switch to underwear brings the final click to the potty puzzle and it's worth the gamble. If your child is overly cautious about change or risks, you may have to lead the way. Just be sure you're ready to live with the consequences. You will need to be a positive, supportive hands-on potty partner if you make the switch and your child is not ready, willing, and able to go it alone.

> Children potty trained before disposable diapers (or who wore cloth diapers) could readily feel the effects of pooping and peeing in their diaper. Diapers got wet, droopy, and markedly heavy. The post-potty experience was distinct from the pre-potty experience, which easily motivated some children to experiment with holding their pee and poop to relieve in other places.

Pull-Ups

If your child is interested in underwear but is not yet ready, you can try potty training pull-ups. Some children will be attracted to the newness of the experience as well as to the child-friendly design. Potty training pull-ups are fun interest-generating tools for potty training. They can also increase your child's self awareness by giving him visual or sensory cues when he potties in his diaper.

Keep in mind the biggest challenge to potty training is your child knowing beforehand that it's time to use the potty. Potty training pull-ups cannot create physical control where none exists. They can assist you in the potty process but you still need a potty plan to guide your child through to mastery.

Potty training will always be the push and pull between convenience and mess. Accidents may be messy but they are the mistakes that teach. Although you may choose convenience, there are no shortcuts.

Letting Go of Diapers

Some children have strong emotional attachments to their diapers, even after they are potty trained. Keep things low key to prevent an escalating power struggle. Affirm the positive—"I know one day you'll tell me when you want to wear your underwear." Indeed, he will decide one day that he's had enough time with diapers.

Accept your child's preference while gently encouraging the transition to underwear. For example, you might say something light-hearted but without sarcasm, such as "You're the first child I know who uses the potty but still likes to wear a diaper."

Try to verbalize what he thinks are the advantages of diapers over underwear. Talk about the diapers having soft thick padding whereas underwear is made of thin material. Experiment with short intervals in underwear if he agrees. Sing the "Big Underwear" song by Joe Scruggs.

If your child is young and the diaper isn't creating any problems at school, your child will conquer this problem in his own time. The awareness of same-age peers is also a natural incentive. However, if you believe your child needs your help because the diaper is increasingly a source of embarrassment or frustration, slowly prepare him for a change. Let him know that on a particular day, you aren't buying any more diapers. Let your child participate in a countdown to the date by marking off calendar days or by seeing the number of diapers get smaller and smaller. Then he can prepare himself for the inevitable leap into underwear.

Sometimes children completely understand the potty process, and may have even had some initial success peeing in the potty, when they decide they are not ready to poop in the potty. If your child asks you to put on his diaper so he can poop in it, support this need. Acknowledge that your child understands how his body works. Trust that he knows what he needs.

You can give him the emotional security of his diaper while building his confidence. Give him a verbal affirmation—"I know it feels better to poop in the diaper for now and I know you will tell me when you don't need it anymore."

Continue with your typical bathroom routine. Empty the diaper into the toilet and let him flush the toilet if he wants. Continue to let him wipe himself and wash his own hands.

If your child is older and more verbal, he may be able to explain what he likes about the diaper and what he does not like about the potty. Once you have that information, you can help find a solution to his dilemma. Given respectful support for his decision, your child will willingly give up the diaper when he no longer needs it.

Your child's potty learning style is exactly right for your child. Chase all your doubts aside. This will have a perfectly positive outcome. With more playful strategies ahead, you can continue to support your child's learning with joy.

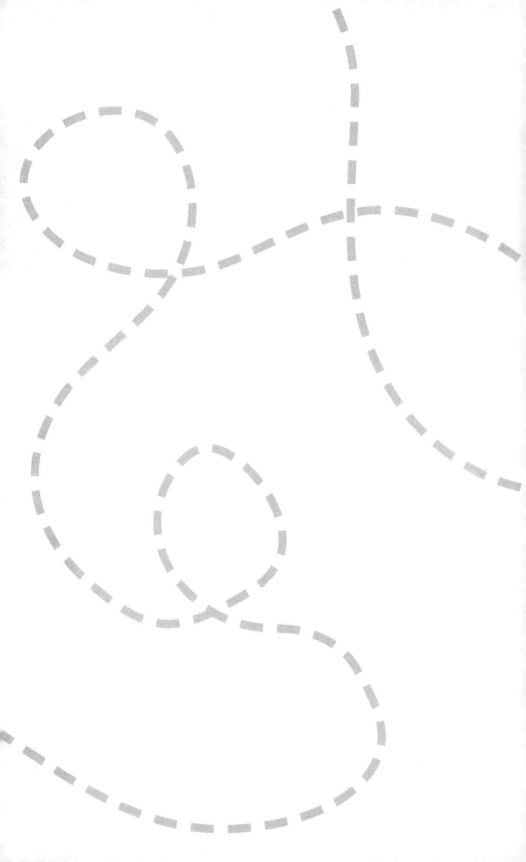

7

Playful Potty Strategies

If all children learn best through play, your child learns best through her favorite kind of play. Some children are happiest in wide open spaces while others could play contentedly in a cozy corner. Some children get lost in pretend activities while others want to take apart real objects and see how they work. You want to pick playful potty strategies based on your child's genuine interests and personality.

Individual Personalities and Interests

The Doer

A physically precocious child likes to do first and reflect afterwards. Appeal to her sense of adventure and need for action. Keep her body busy and you will engage her mind; ignore her body and she will be bored and distracted. Because potty training requires self-awareness, you must hook the verbal-cognitive message onto predictable actions.

Play beat the clock to get to the bathroom as fast as she can, give "high fives" if she makes it to the potty, or do an "end zone potty dance" (or try all three). This is the child of "big action," so don't slow her down with buttons and zippers. Your potty training style has to be quick and to the point.

The Talker

A talkative child has abundant language and loves explanations. She listens to the potty training plan and rephrases each step in her own words. She repeats key phrases to remind herself what to do next, and gains control over her action by talking. If you are a parent with similar verbal strengths, this is easy and natural for you. If you have other strengths, your child's need for talking may drive you a little crazy.

Read and discuss potty books and stories with your child. You can talk about your potty plans when she wakes up in the morning and talk about today's potty adventures before bed at night. You might want to stand outside the bathroom door and listen as she sings or talks to herself through each and every potty time. Pay attention to the words she uses; you may need to borrow from your child's verbal repertoire at another time.

The Thinker

A mini-intellectual loves figuring out how things work. She may be one of those children that seem wise beyond her years. She enjoys working on logical puzzles, sorting, sequencing, matching, and counting. She may also love books and self-designed science projects, especially figuring out where the poop goes when you flush the toilet.

Play games with your child that organize and collect vital potty facts. For example, how many potty candles were collected today for her celebration cake? And is that number more or less than yesterday?

This potty-goer might prefer potty sequence cards instead of a less challenging potty photo book. You can make a stack of potty action cards and let your little thinker arrange in temporal and logical order: (1) diaper wearing; (2) open bathroom door; (3) take off pants; (4) sit on potty; (5) look at a book while on potty; (6) wipe tushie; (7) flush toilet; (8) put on pants; (9) wash hands; (10) high five. Start with five actions, and then add more.

The Performer

An imaginative child excels at imitation and pretend play. She is observant, engaged, and attuned to the rich details of everyday actions. She may embellish play with narrative themes or characters. Your little performer might assume new identities or invite imaginary friends into her potty adventure.

Incorporate themes from her favorite stories into your potty training strategies. She will be interested to hear whether her favorite characters are using diapers or underwear. Fictional characters are her dear friends who can be part of her potty learning adventure. Rehearsing those potty training skills in pretend play is her personal actor's studio.

The Socialite

A little social butterfly makes eye contact easily, encouraging social connections, like any great politician. She initiates and welcomes social interaction. She'll happily be the last to leave the party. She learns best with others rather than alone.

Base your potty training strategies on the motto "the more the merrier!" She's the child who wants a hands-on potty partner to hold her hand on the way to the potty and to share her successes. Line up all her favorite potty role models, real and fictitious. This little party girl is motivated by people. Call all her very important people with potty updates. She'll join the club if you can show her they're waiting for her grand entrance. She's ready for a potty party!

Playful Potty Books, Videos, and Songs

Books and music are two universally engaging activities for potty going age children, regardless of individual personalities. They appeal to all the personality types: the doer, the talker, the thinker, the performer, and the socialite. You simply have to pick the stories and the songs that fit your child's natural strengths. Fun potty videos are also a great way to reinforce a positive potty message.

Playful Potty Books

Many children love to read on the potty, especially if they have potty reading role models. Your child is imitating you. Reading may help her sit on the potty longer. Keep a basket of books, catalogues, and old mail next to her potty. But also let her know that potty reading is a means to an end and not an end in itself.

> Set a foundation for potty training when your child is a young toddler. When you talk about the dog peeing, the cat pooping, or the bird poop on the sidewalk, think of this as a toddler science lesson. You are building a meaningful context for your child's future potty learning.

Allow your child to sit on the potty with her books as long as she wants during the "making friends with the potty" stage. This is the time when your child is building familiarity with the fit and feel of her potty. Once she has that confidence and she understands the purpose of sitting on the potty, give her gentle reminders of why she's there. For example, "I'm listening but I don't hear the pee pee." It's okay to wait for a poop or a pee, but you don't want her sitting there reading indefinitely. Distinguish between playing on the potty and purposeful potty behavior. For example, you might say, "Let's go read in your chair and we'll come back when you're ready to pee."

Like adults, different children will connect with different books. Your child might connect with the image of a little-girl queen using the potty. Your child might want the silliest potty book in the world while another child wants an emotionally triumphant potty adventure. Take your time to find your child's favorite.

A few meaningful books at your child's fingertips are one more way of giving your child power and ownership over her potty experiences. There are many great potty books that you can share with your child. Here are some favorites:

- *A Potty for Me!* by Karen Katz
- *Does a Pig Flush?* by Fred Ehrlich
- *Everyone Poops* by Taro Gomi
- *Go, Girl! Go Potty!* by Harriet Ziefert Inc.
- *Going on the Potty* by Fred Rogers
- *I Have to Go!* by Robert Munsch
- *Lift the Lid, Use the Potty* by Annie Ingle and Lisa McCue
- *No More Diapers for Ducky* by Bernette Ford and Sam Williams
- *No Potty! Yes, Potty!* by Harriet Ziefert Inc.
- *Once Upon a Potty* by Alona Frankel
- *The Prince and the Potty* by Wendy Cheyette Lewison
- *The Princess and the Potty* by Wendy Cheyette Lewison
- *The Potty Book for Boys* by Alyssa Satin Capucilli
- *The Potty Book for Girls* by Alyssa Satin Capucilli
- *Time to Pee* by Mo Willems
- *Uh Oh! Gotta Go! Potty Tales from Toddlers* by Bob McGrath
- *What Do You Do with a Potty* by Marianne Borgardt
- *Where's the Poop* by Julie Markes and Susan Kathleen Hartung
- *You Can Go to the Potty* by William Sears, M.D., Martha Sears, R.N., and Christie Watts Kelly
- *Your New Potty* by Joanna Cole

Playful Potty Videos

Potty videos are another way of reinforcing a positive potty message for your child. Your child will identify with her favorite characters in these videos, sharing their potty adventures, and learning from their potty struggles. Again, be selective. Pick the video that matches your child's interests. Here are a few favorite potty videos:

- *Bear in the Big Blue House* by Martin Hugh Mitchell
- *I Can Go Potty* by Mazzarella Productions
- *It's Potty Time* by Learning Through Entertainment, Inc.
- *Let's Go Potty* by Dr. Betti Hertzberg
- *Once Upon a Potty for her* by Alona Frankel
- *Once Upon a Potty for him* by Alona Frankel

Playful Potty Music

Music helps your child internalize the positive potty message in the same hands-on way as books and videos. Singing routine potty songs also reinforces positive potty training routines. You can use songs in a variety of ways to playfully engage your potty training child during transition times; to help an active child sit still; to focus your child on a specific potty skill (like hand washing or walking to the bathroom at night); and to give emotional encouragement.

Pick songs that you are happy singing over and over. Learn one or two that make you smile, and enjoy the silliness of being a potty training partner! Here are a few musical favorites:

- *Miss Joanie's Potty Party* by Joanie Whitaker
- *The Once Upon a Potty—Potty Songs CD* by Ari Frankel
- *Potty Animal: Funny Songs about Potty Training* by Auntie Poo & The Porta-Potties
- *Potty Song: customized potty training song* at www.pottysong.com
- *Potty Song 1, Potty Song 2, and Potty Song 3* (free potty songs) on www.PottyTrainingConcepts.com

- *Tinkle, Tinkle, Little Tot: Songs and Rhymes for Toilet Training* (book) by Bruce Lansky, Robert Pottle, and Friends

The best songs, of course, are the ones you or your child makes up in the potty moment. Combine her name and potty actions with any favorite tune. She will be singing and dancing her way right out of those diapers.

Creating a Personal Potty Book

Your child's personal "My Potty Book" is *her* potty story. The more specific it is to her needs and her journey, the more perfect it is. Your child loves looking at herself. A personal potty book helps your potty-age child build a positive self-image as a potty-goer.

Photo books increase your child's self-awareness. She can reflect on the images and think, "Aha, that's what I look like." She might discover that the potty isn't so big, or she might feel pride sitting on the potty reading her book or seeing herself flushing the toilet, remembering that it was a little scary the first time.

Photo books increase your child's potty comprehension. Books are tangible. It's easier to remember the potty sequence when you see it in a book in front of you. A photo book takes abstract potty choices and makes them concrete for your child. Your child can read her potty photo book any time and anywhere—when she's happy, proud, frustrated, sad, or confused. She can read it alone or with someone else. Books have power. A potty photo-book gives your child power to conquer any potty situation.

Instructions

1. Take six to ten potty-related photos (suggestions below). If you have more pictures that you want to include, divide them into two different potty-themed books. You want each book to be

short and sweet. Here are some suggestions for pictures and captions. However, feel free to customize your books your way:

  a. A picture of your child wearing a diaper ("Once upon a time I wore a diaper.")

  b. A picture of your child playing ("I can feel it when I need to use the potty.")

  c. A picture of your child going into the bathroom—waving, smiling, and generally acting it up ("Got to go!" or "Got to go. Now!")

  d. A picture of your child sitting on the potty ("I feel good.")

  e. A picture of your child washing her hands ("Happy potty to me . . .")

  f. A picture of you kissing, hugging, or high-five-ing your child ("Yeah, I did it!")

  g. Additional pictures might be of different bathrooms, the potty without your child on it, a teddy bear on the potty, friends and family cheering for your child, or an artistic still life of underpants on display on a clothesline or in an interesting arrangement on the bed.

2. Paste or print your pictures on heavy card stock paper.

3. Write or print your captions. Fewer words are better for these young readers.

4. Decorate the book with stickers or designs, if desired.

5. Laminate it at your local office store.

6. The "My Potty Book" is to be well read and well loved. Your child's book will become worn and battered. Make two if you want a keepsake to put away. You should also make additional copies to keep at a grandparent's or babysitter's home.

Praise and Rewards

Praise is sincere positive feedback you give your child when she does something well, makes good choices, or strives to learn a new skill—even if there's still more to learn. Praise tells your child that she really is on the right course to accomplish what she set out to do. Praise has an important place in a playful potty environment.

When giving praise, remember to be sincere. Everyone knows that the words "good job" lose meaning faster than "have a nice day." And keep in mind that this is about your child learning a skill according to her own pace.

Similarly tricky is the use of rewards, the tangible tokens commemorating your child's accomplishments. Most children love getting stuff. The problem is that potty-age children do not always remember the symbolism of the gesture. They get hooked on the stuff and forget that this toy or those candies were about making good potty choices. Your child may see the reward as an end in itself. And before you know it, what started as a positive reward may feel more like a desperate bribe.

Potty play time emphasizes your child's accomplishments in every shape and form. Instead of the stuff, she will look forward to time with you. Using the potty is the reward that announces "Hooray for ME!" and "I did it!" Potty play times reinforce a positive potty partnership and the thrill of success.

If you incorporate games and songs into potty training that capture your child's interest, you won't need external rewards. Potty training can be a positive experience by itself. A variety of fun and effective potty training games and songs are discussed in the next chapter.

Stickers and Charts

Stickers and charts can be positive ways to record and reward your child's growing skill at pottying. You can make a weekly poster from poster board with long column spaces for daily stickers counting your child's potty times (see the following chart). Let your child put a sticker on her chart when she uses the potty. Your child's active participation in a sticker activity is her personal announcement that "I did it!"

This activity can also be done by drawing "potty stars" using whiteboard markers and a whiteboard or chalk and a chalkboard. Whichever you may choose, keep the chart in the bathroom for immediate follow-through.

Monday	Tuesday	Wednesday	Thursday	Friday	Saturday	Sunday

A potty chart is better as a child-directed activity than as a parent reward system because it gives your child personal ownership over her success. An external expectation to "earn" stickers or "potty stars" can create the same power struggles as token rewards and praise.

One of the problems with stickers is that they lose their effectiveness when the novelty wears off. They are fun at first because they are new and children love the attention. Sticker charts are meaningful when they support your child's interest versus when the charts are intended to generate interest. For example, if your child is striving to be potty proficient, the sticker chart is a concrete record of getting closer and closer to her goal.

Smart children, who are not potty motivated, realize fairly early that they have other options. This creates an opportunity for a power struggle—similar to when you offer your child a choice of blue or red and your child picks green. At some point, your child figures out that it's not about stickers at all but about something else that she doesn't really want to do. And she rebels.

Honor her choice and wait on the potty training until she has an interest that will sustain her through the training process. You will enjoy it more and so will she.

Food as a Reward

You may hear potty stories from parents who kept bowls of candy in the bathroom to reward potty successes. Food rewards won't work for all children, especially children who are not ready for potty training. And you certainly want to be careful about any underlying messages that food might be an emotional fix-all.

Food can be a positive ingredient in family rituals and celebrations. Focus on the event and the joy of being together. Plan a trip out for ice cream or make homemade sundaes with lots of different toppings on potty play days. It's one thing to teach children the spirit of generosity by giving them things they like; it's another to withhold what they like unless they do something you want. Potty training cannot be conditional—that will only teach your child to perform on demand. Your goal is to teach your child to understand and trust her body.

Using food as a reward can have negative consequences. Children can begin to make emotional connections to food that can follow them into their adult lives. As with other token rewards, children can easily confuse the piece of candy as the goal instead of the "Hooray for me—look what I can do!" Your child is not being trained to do "tricks." If she could learn to walk without the lure of treats, she can also feel proud and capable in her body without token treats. Potty training is prime time to concentrate on your child's positive attitude about her emotions and her body.

Potty Training Complications

If simplicity works in your favor, life's complications work against your child's success. Changes can unsettle your child. But also keep in mind that your child experiences her world up-close and personal. So, for example, travel might throw off her sleep schedule but having her favorite teddy bear and hearing her special lullaby make everything alright. Here are a few situations that may complicate your child's potty training experience.

New Baby Sibling

A new baby in the house takes away time-consuming support from your child's potty efforts and presents the confusing impression that babies get all the attention. In the big picture, welcoming a new sibling takes priority over potty training. If your child is ready and interested and you still have months before the baby arrives, go for it. But watch out for the pressure of finishing "on time." It's better to set a solid foundation than to scramble to be completely finished potty training. These tips will help you after baby arrives:

- Make a photo book for your older child so she can read about herself as a baby after the new baby arrives. Include pictures of her on the potty and a picture of her diaper and potty chair next to baby's tiny little diaper and changing table.
- Avoid authoritarian commands when giving your potty-age child potty reminders. Even though you will be busier with the new baby, you don't want your older child to feel rushed. Choose playful phrases like "okay little bunny, let me see you hop to the bathroom."

• Attend to your older child first before feeding or changing the baby. Five minutes with your two year old can buy you twenty uninterrupted minutes with your newborn.

New Bed

It's usually a good idea to introduce one change at a time. Changing your child's sleep routine from the crib to a bed requires another dimension of independence. Let your child master each one separately. If your toddler is climbing out of her crib, you will probably be moving her into the bed before structured potty training begins. If you have a mellow child who sleeps happily in her crib, daytime potty training can begin while she's still in the crib. Keep in mind it may be months or a year between completing daytime potty training and completing nighttime potty training.

• Be prepared not worried. Draw on your playful attitude to calmly explain what your child should do in case of a potty-time. Any anxiety on your part influences your child's confidence.

• Use familiar bedtime routines to create consistency. Your potty-age child does best mastering one new thing at a time.

• Expect the unexpected. Regressions are opportunities to go back to re-integrate new skills slowly.

Vacations

Traveling can disrupt well-established schedules and routines. Active potty training requires consistent routines and often familiar locations. At the same time, it isn't realistic to delay all travel until potty training is complete. Simply evaluate travel arrangements and schedules from your child's point of view. Her physical needs and this new skill trumps all other adult conveniences. You want to be well prepared for accidents and creative potty solutions.

Now is the time when all those personal potty routines pay off. Songs and games that can be adapted on the road give your child comfort and confidence. Try to maintain as much consistency as possible with your home routine. Have a plan for your child's predictable potty needs as well as the unpredictable ones.

- Schedule flights and layover times accordingly.
- Carry extra clothes, extra pull-ups, and possibly a folding potty seat or a travel potty chair.
- Plan for potty breaks every two hours, and give your child ongoing encouragement and reminders of the new routine.
- Use diapers to prevent accidents when potties will be unavailable for long periods of time. Diapers alone will not create regression.

Moving

Moving to a new house means lots more to do, as well as changes to the routines and the familiarity of the environment. If the move is less than a month away, do not start potty training. You have too many other things to do. Better to use any available free time to hang out with your child, in between packing, that is. Forestall the potty training agenda but continue to immerse her in a positive potty environment by talking, playing, watching, pretending, and joking. A little attention a few times a day reinforces your potty training momentum. You can start more structured potty training after your child has adjusted to the move, in two to four weeks.

- Make a "My Two Houses" photo book for your child, including photos of his old bedroom, yard and neighbors, and a photo of your child using the potty in his old bathroom. Add pictures of the new house after you arrive.
- Play "same and different," talking about all the ways it's the same to potty in a new house and all the ways it's different. Notice the details: the toilet paper holder, the color of the bathroom walls, the underwear your child is wearing.
- Play "count the bathrooms." Does your child potty in many bathrooms? Where's the first bathroom your child learned to potty? How many bathrooms are there in the whole world?

● ● ●

Any changes that draw energy and effort away from your child will impact potty training, including new jobs, new schools, family stresses. Changes are also opportunities to practice your playful potty training creativity. You will decide whether the situation warrants postponing potty training for a short period of time or creating flexible engaging adaptations that support your child's progress through the temporary disruptions. Be realistic about what you can and can't do. The best choice is the one that is the least stressful for your family.

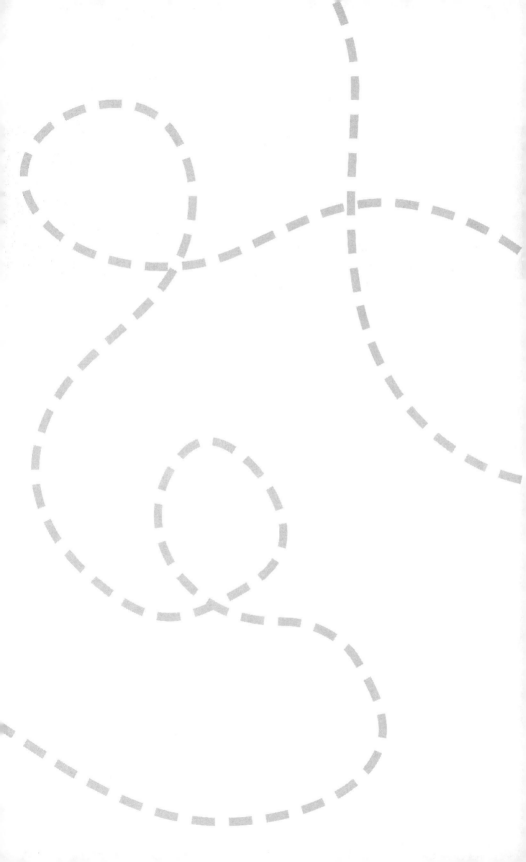

Playful Potty Games

8

Children love games. They also learn new skills more easily with games. Playful potty training employs games to make the learning process as significant as the ultimate potty skills. It's not just what you learn that's important, it's how you learn. Games that tap into the natural interests and abilities of children celebrate each age and stage of childhood. Silliness and movement, magical stories, pretend dramas, secret signals, and happy celebrations all make potty training come alive to a child. Potty games are a way to keep your child involved, not merely a way to keep him busy or distracted. They are strategies to fully engage him in the potty learning experience in a way that makes sense to him.

Repetition is important to a good potty game. If your child enjoys a particular game, stick with it. Incorporate that game into each potty experience. From making each potty visit fun to alleviating the stress of potty accidents, potty games can be very effective personalized potty rituals.

Bathroom Games

Some children need a little playful help to slow down and tune in to their bodies. Here are a few games to engage your child while he is sitting on the potty. Use them to buy him some time to be successful—not as a distraction from his ultimate potty-going purpose. Remember to avoid power struggles and let your child leave the potty if he's not interested.

"I Spy"

Take turns noticing something that's in the bathroom while the other person guesses what it is. End with "Do I spy something in the potty? Yes, I do!"

"I Hear"

Take turns listening to sounds you hear from in the bathroom, in the house, outside the bathroom window. Guess what the other person hears. End with "Do I hear something in the potty? Yes, I do!"

Sing Potty Songs

Sing a favorite potty song just long enough to see "if the pee or the pop is ready to come out." Here's one adapted from "Here We Go Round the Mulberry Bush":

This is the way we sit on the potty,
Sit on the potty, sit on the potty,
This is the way we sit on the potty
Early in the morning
(Every afternoon/early in the ev'ning/before we go to bed)

Here's one to the tune of "Frere Jacques":

Are you peeing? Are you peeing?
Little one, little one.

Yes, I am. Yes, I am.
Now I'm done. Now I'm done.

Tell a Potty Story

Here's one called "Fast Boy" about a little boy who couldn't sit still. You can customize your own potty story based on your child's interests and potty particulars. Some ideas for story themes are "when daddy was a little boy learning to potty"; "the dinosaur that was too big for the bathroom"; "the splashing toilet that no one would sit on"; and "the perfect toilet seat (not too big and not too small; not too hard and not too soft)."

Once upon a time there was a little boy who everyone called "fast boy." He was fast, fast, fast—always running and jumping, never sitting still. When he wanted to learn to use the potty, he would fly in and out of the bathroom so fast. He flew right over his potty. His mommy had to think of some way to help him sit long enough to use the potty. Fast boy's mommy talked to the queen of the bees who had many fast little bees. Queen bee gave fast boy's mommy a special sticky potion that would catch fast boy on his potty. And from now on fast boy's mommy always covers fast boy's potty with the mixture from the bees. Do you feel it? I think there's some on your potty right now.

Collect Toilet Paper Rolls

The more you potty, the faster you empty the toilet paper roll. Start a basket of empty toilet paper rolls. Older children can guess how long it will take to go through a roll of toilet paper. You can have a contest to see who uses the last bit of toilet paper. The last person has to toot the toilet paper horn when they finish a roll. Use the empty rolls for tunnels for small cars or paint with them.

Aiming Games for Boys

Accurate aim is another potty skill that requires focus and coordination. It comes with experience. Well, sort of. Practice may not make perfect but at least you can make it more fun. Sometimes you can improve aim just by sitting your child backwards on the regular bathroom toilet. Otherwise try some of these classic adaptations.

Sink the Cheerio

Add a few cheerios to the toilet when your child is learning to pee standing. Tell him to aim for the cheerio and try to sink it.

Blue + Yellow = Green

Squirt a few drops of blue food coloring into the water. Tell your child to watch what happens when yellow pee mixes with blue food coloring.

Bulls-Eye

Buy commercial tissue paper targets. These come in animal shapes, construction, and transportation themes. Whether it's store-bought or homemade, your child will enjoy taking control of his body.

Potty Success Games

When your child's potty success is in his own hands, you eliminate emotional power struggles from the potty training experience. He's in charge of his own body. He's in charge of becoming more independent. These games make your child's success concrete and tangible. He can see his own achievements and be proud of himself.

Red Light, Green Light

Laminate red and green cards that your child can put into a deco-rated tissue box in the bathroom. You can also cut red and green shapes from foam sheets available in craft stores. He can put a "green light" in the box if he went potty or a "red light" if he did not. You can also use smaller red light/green light cards with Velcro on a bathroom poster board.

High Five

Make a handprint of your child's hand on a bathroom tile or poster with the words "High Five." After your child sits on the potty, he can stop to give himself a high five.

"I Did It" Board

Make an "I did it" wall poster. You can make columns for days of the week or columns for each member of the family. Your child can record his potty times with a potty sticker on his personal potty poster. This also works using a whiteboard using dry-erase markers.

Clang! Clang!

Place a bell in your child's potty place. After sitting on the potty, he can ring the bell—like those bartenders who ring the bell when they receive a big tip. Of course, everyone in the house should cheer loudly when they hear the bell ringing!

Potty Photo Wall

Create a photo wall of happy potty pictures. Take pictures of your child using the potty at home, at the store, in restaurant bath-rooms, at his grandparent's house, and his friend's house. Your child is building an image of himself as a full-time, anywhere, everywhere potty-goer.

Ice Cream Party

Celebrate potty play days by letting your child eat ice cream sundaes. If your child is spending potty play days undressed, why not have a little celebration before putting his clothes back on! You won't have to worry about dripping ice cream.

Cleanup Games

Believe it or not, children like to clean—if cleanup is a game. The most effective strategy is to be ready *before* the accidents happen and eliminate the "uh-oh" factor. Place the cleanup supplies in a convenient location and teach your child how to be helpful. Gently supervise until he knows the boundaries between helpful and not-so helpful. Generally speaking, if your child is making an effort, it's helpful—although you may need to stand near with an extra towel. Continue to encourage good hand-washing and let your child spray-clean after you pick up the poop accidents.

Squirt Away

Spray bottles always make cleanup more fun. Buy a small spray bottle that fits your child's small hands. Practice outside or on mirrors with plain water. Be sure to fill with a nontoxic, child-friendly cleaner.

Sing a Cleanup Song

Sing one you already know or invent a new potty version. Here's one to the tune of "Old Mc Donald." Substitute your child's name for David:

Little David cleaned the mess
E-I-E-I-O
With a wipe wipe here and a wipe wipe there
E-I-E-I-O

Little David cleaned the mess
E-I-E-I-O
Choose words to fit any situation:
Little David sprayed the spray.
Little David wiped the floor.
Little David pitched the trash.

Feed the Trash Animal

Buy an inexpensive plastic wastebasket with a flip-flap cover and draw a "hungry" face on the flap. Name your potty "trash-eating" animal.

Underwear Games

Underwear is fun and funny. Take advantage of potty training time to cultivate your underwear-themed repertoire. Celebrate wearing underwear with enthusiasm. Let your playfulness reinforce the idea that saying goodbye to diapers is fun. Who knows, you may be creating a family-time ritual that will last for years. An underwear dance party or parade could be the perfect grand finale for your child's ultimate potty success.

Underwear Books

Add the books *Underwear!* by Mary Elise Monsell and Lynn Munsinger or *What Color Is Your Underwear?* by Sam Lloyd to your home library. Congratulate your child as he becomes a member of the underwear-wearing club.

Underwear Party

Buy extra-large underwear for the whole family to wear over clothes or even on their heads. Plan a weekly underwear party where everyone wears underwear to a normal family routine like dinner time, game time, or story time. Or check out a clown supply retailer for the "world's largest underwear" that the whole family can wear, at the same time.

Underwear Dancing

Collect your favorite dance songs for daily "underwear dancing." An underwear favorite is Joe Scruggs singing "Big Underwear," available on the *Ants* CD.

Underwear Parade

Wave high-flying flags with silly underwear as you march around the house chanting:

Goodbye diapers.

Goodbye diapers.

Goodbye diapers.

Don't need you anymore!

So long diapers.

So long diapers.

So long diapers.

I'm going to the store!

Hello underwear.

Hello underwear.

Hello underwear.

It's you I do adore!

Wait! Before you get too excited about your diaper finale, there are still more playful potty ideas to help your child love potty training.

Potty Pretend

9

Potty pretend play is one of the best ways for your child to integrate new concepts into future behavior. When your child pretends, she tries on new roles to see if she likes them and can practice skills without worrying about mistakes. She can problem-solve her way through potty fears and potty mistakes in a variety of different potty scenarios using dolls, teddy bears, books, songs, and videos. You might, for example, hear your child reminding her bear to "take your time and listen for the pee" or acting out a page from her favorite potty book. Each time she repeats the scenario, she is thinking aloud using her whole body. Give your child the opportunity to playfully reenact potty behavior, and you help build confidence and competence.

Don't forget that the pretend world is merely an extension of reality to your potty-age child. Imagination stretches your child's thinking, making it easier to maneuver around more complex concepts like potty training. It also gives your child a special power in a big adult world. Take advantage of this vital tool to help your child face the age-appropriate, but very adult, demands of potty training.

Supervising Pretend Play

Although she may be taking the lead, remember to casually supervise your child's play potty situations. It helps to remind your child of the difference between real and pretend, and the difference between a play potty and the real potty that your child uses in the bathroom. You don't want your child really peeing on the doll's play potty, and you don't want the teddy bear sitting in real pee. If something like this does happen, treat it as any potty accident. Stay calm. Explain what's okay and what's not okay. Fix the problem and end on a positive note. If your child is confused between real and pretend, feel free to remove the play props until a later time when your child understands the difference.

Potty Training Dolls

Children who are learning to make the connection between what comes out of their body and what goes into the potty may enjoy seeing a potty doll that actually pees in the potty. Potty training dolls, available from most retail potty supply outlets, teach children the immediate cause and effect connection between drinking and peeing. Some dolls pee immediately after drinking while others do not pee until their stomach is pressed.

When deciding whether to introduce a potty training doll, consider your individual child. What does your child understand about her own body and other potty role models? Does she already understand the connection between pee and potties? Decide whether you need a potty training doll to make a literal connection to the potty or whether your child's imagination with an ordinary doll will do the trick.

Role-Playing Scenarios

If your child has questions or concerns about potty training, they will probably show up in her play scenarios. Role play can help her practice letting go of the security of diapers, face the anxiety of not getting to the potty in time, and create a safe transition from a potty chair to a toilet seat. Here are a few role-play scenarios that allow your child to play both the teacher and the student in the potty training process.

> You can let your child pretend by holding a doll or teddy bear on the potty. Listen to how your child speaks to the doll to get a glimpse of what he's thinking.

Potty Pretend

Create a pretend bathroom space. Set up potty props like a toy potty chair and toy sink area on a small area rug or use a large cardboard box to build a play bathroom. Let your child pretend holding a doll or teddy bear on the potty. Listen to how she speaks to the doll or bear to get a glimpse of what she's thinking. You can even create a mini version with a small box and a few Weebles.

Pretend Diaper Changing Station

Buy real baby-size diapers. Set up a pretend diaper changing station where your child can re-experience the pleasure of diapers with a doll or bear. Although your child is leaving her diapers behind, she can relive her emotional connection to diapers through play.

Puppets

Use hand puppets, finger puppets, or spoon puppets to have a conversation about potty training. At first, you can speak for the mommy and the child puppets, telling a story about a little girl who was learning to use the potty. In time, you and your child can switch roles and incorporate any new potty themes that arise in your home.

Books and Stories

Extend your child's favorite potty stories and songs into everyday play situations. Retell the stories from books and videos while you're driving in the car or walking to the store. Potty training comprehension increases with every retelling.

Potty Shtick

Here's where you create a comic potty routine worthy of a vaudeville stage. The routine starts with what sounds very serious but it's all about the big laughs. Here's one possible shtick about a child who is capable of potty training but still holding out for reasons known only to her. Your stories will surely be even better.

Parent, pretending to be on the phone to the preschool teacher, to grandparents, to the mailman, to Mickey Mouse, to any of the characters in your child's life:

"Hello, I'd like to introduce ____. She's wonderful and smart but there's one thing she will never ever do while she's with you. I know she's not going to use the potty before she starts college.

Yes, of course, we bought a potty chair.

Yes, of course, she eats real food and drinks water.

Yes, I know, I know you know lots of children who use the potty before college.

But my child is s-p-e-c-i-a-l. She says she's going to invent diapers that fit kids who go to school. She'll be famous. You watch."

Then look in the crystal ball at your child's future birthday parties and try to peek to see if she's still wearing underwear.

Count off birthdays up to eighteen years. Saying "no, not yet" for each year.

Finish by asking your child which birthday will be the one. This is all in good fun. If your child says "twelfth birthday," teasingly ask "are you sure?"

Potty pretend should always be focused on your child having fun while she's learning new potty skills. The rules for pretend are the same as the rules for play—your child decides on the "rules" because your child knows best how the play situation fits her needs at this particular time.

Potty Training Themes

Potty training themes capture a child's interest and curiosity. Themes add a personal connection to her potty adventure, creating a special place that she shares with favorite characters and familiar experiences. You can incorporate your child's favorite themes into potty training with bathroom accessories, dolls and animals, even with seemingly two-dimensional posters or wall decorations. These themes provide the prompts to talk about and generate new potty play experiences. Your child's imagination will lead the way.

Potty play themes can be developmental or based on your child's particular interests. Potty-age children are taking the monumental leap out of babyhood into childhood, so "growing" is a major developmental theme during the potty years. Does Mickey Mouse wear diapers? Maybe he did but now he wears pants. Is the potty chair just like a throne for a king or a queen? Your child will be naturally drawn to the themes that meet her current needs: trust, confidence, security, power, and control, to name a few. Whether the theme characters are "old friends" who are cheering on their little potty learner or jungle animals imparting messages to keep trying, your child is not alone in her potty adventure.

If your child has a favorite character from a book or movie, include that character in your potty discussions and pretend play. Don't worry if her interest borders on obsession. She will relinquish her attachment to a special character when that particular need has been met.

Potty-age children might be attracted to dinosaurs or big, strong animals to show them how to be fearless. Or they might be drawn to little kittens that are kept clean by mommy cats. Potty pretend themes are a window to your child's heart. Take a peek. Imagination is always more powerful than logic to the new potty-goer.

Practice and Imitation

Repetition builds mastery. Every time your child hears the same story read again or asks to wear the same clothes over and over, she is asserting her control in a sometimes unpredictable world. Through potty pretend play, your child is able to repeat going to the potty until she is completely satisfied with every nuance of the experience. Like the well-practiced tennis swing, your child's potty behavior will become more automatic after repeated rehearsals.

> Childhood imagination is essential to in-depth learning. Give it time and space to emerge. Your child's experience will be enhanced by the creativity, problem solving, and pure joy that transforms the ordinary into the extraordinary.

Continue to be a playful potty role model. As long as your child is actively unraveling the mysteries of potty training, you are needed as a hands-on potty partner. Stay tuned in to your child's needs and questions. Be ready to add supportive potty experiences or just some potty silliness.

Most importantly, give your child as much time as she needs to own her potty training experience. Active potty training may last a few days or a few weeks, but for the majority of children, potty training is a learning process that involves months of playful work.

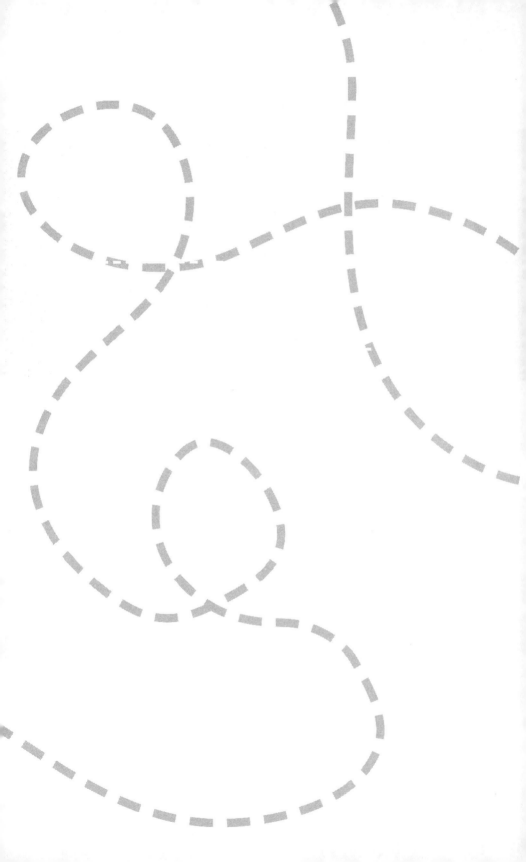

Part Three

All Day, All Night

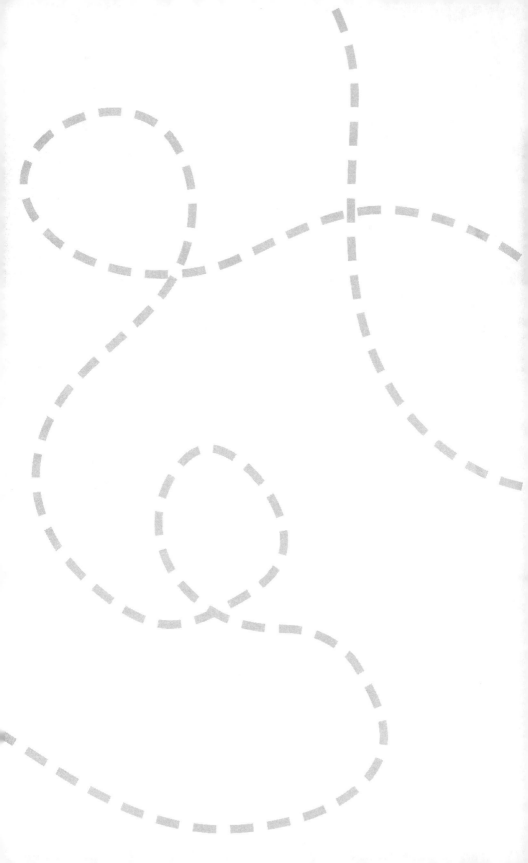

10

Nighttime Magic

Potty-trained-by-day is not a guarantee of potty-trained-at night. Nighttime potty training is, for many children, a separate venture. It adds two new components to the readiness list: the ability to stay dry through the night (a much longer period of time than in daytime potty training); and the ability to wake up to potty.

These nighttime readiness factors are physiological. Interest, desire, and sheer determination will not give your child the physical ability to stay dry at night or to wake up from a deep sleep. According to the American Academy of Pediatrics, nighttime potty mastery may not occur until four or five years of age. You should speak to your pediatrician if you have any concerns about your child's unique

> Many children are potty trained during the day long before being potty trained at night. Readiness for daytime potty training is not a sign that your child is ready for nighttime potty training. The sign to start nighttime potty training is seeing your child wake up with dry diapers on a regular basis.

situation. Also, check with your pediatrician if your child starts having nighttime accidents after six months of nighttime mastery.

Playful nighttime potty strategies can support your child as he puts together the new pieces of the nighttime potty puzzle. Awareness, control, and interest all work hand-in-hand for nighttime success. If your child is a deep sleeper, he won't have the awareness. If he doesn't realize the need soon enough, he may not have the control. If his bedroom is far from the bathroom, he may not have the interest. If you can identify the reason for the nighttime accidents, you'll have a better idea of the solution. You can teach your child what to do when he wakes up and needs to potty, but the awareness of the need to potty and physically waking from a deep sleep may take more time and maturity.

No Stress Nighttime Potty Routine

A thoughtful pre-bedtime routine can eliminate some nighttime potty emergencies. Your routine should complement your child's usual bedtime routine of stories and snuggles with two additional features: monitoring pre-bedtime drinks and a clear plan for post-bedtime potty visits.

Stop drinks a few hours before bedtime. Your potty training child is too young to comprehend the consequence of drinking too much late in the day. And if he understands the connection, he is too young to delay the gratification of enjoying that last glass of water. Make a potty stop the last thing you do before the last good-night kisses. If you have an extended tuck-in routine with multiple stories, you may allow your child one extra trip out of bed. Watch out, however, for hourly requests to use the potty after lights go out. Chances are these requests are not really about pottying, but are clever nighttime stall tactics.

Be clear about what your child should do if he needs to potty. Choose a routine appropriate for his age and abilities. Do you want him to call for you? Do you want him to walk to the bathroom? Which bathroom? Are there any other "rules" to follow, like "get back to bed without any other stops"? Consistency helps your child's body to establish a pattern (if the physical ability is there) and it helps your child act with confidence if he does need to potty after bedtime.

Playful Nighttime Potty Strategies

Your child may wake up with the sensation of needing to potty, but it might still take enormous effort to actually get out of bed, especially when he's small and the room is dark. If he is having difficulty getting out of bed and to the bathroom, there are several playful strategies to help him get to the bathroom in time.

Introduce bathroom games during the day when your child's confidence is higher than in the middle of the night when he's sleepy. The following games focus on something positive instead of the physical discomfort of needing to potty, which can help him get to the bathroom in time. They also give you a way to temporarily lend a helping hand, while empowering your child to move toward nighttime independence. He may need your hands-on support guiding him through the game plan for a few nights before he is ready to act alone.

Follow the Potty Road

Make a masking tape line from your child's bed to the potty. Or, be innovative with colorful painter's tape or make broken or wriggly lines. You could also trace your child's footprints on construction paper. Cut, laminate, and tape a path to follow on the floor from his bed to the potty.

Light the Way

Leave a fun flashlight by your child's bed to shine the way. Or, add a string of "runway" lights along the hallway to the bathroom. Add a Johnny-Light™ to the toilet and your toilet will light green when the toilet lid is up.

Sing Along the Way

Add a favorite walking song to your child's nighttime potty visit or revise a favorite "moon" song to fit your child's nighttime potty walk.

Heigh Ho! Heigh Ho!
It's off to potty I go!
Heigh ho, Heigh ho, Heigh ho,
Heigh ho, Heigh ho, Heigh ho.
Walking, walking
Sh, Sh, Sh,
Sh, Sh, Sh.
Quiet to the potty,
Quiet to the potty,
Sh, Sh, Sh,
Sh, Sh, Sh.

Step by Step

Count the steps from your child's bed to the potty during the day. He can count on the way to the potty and on the way back. Is it the same number every night? Are there more or less steps at night?

Nocturnal Friends

Talk about all the animals that come out at night: smart owls, strong tigers, quiet snakes, noisy crickets, sneaky sharks. Let your child pretend he's one of those animals when he wakes to go potty. Remind him, though, that's it's really not playtime and to go right back to bed. You could give him a nocturnal pet like a gerbil or horseshoe crabs.

No-Fault Nighttime Accidents

Your child may experience nighttime accidents for any number of reasons, ranging from simply forgetting to make that final potty stop before getting into bed to age-appropriate fears about getting out of bed when he needs to potty. Nighttime accidents can be more challenging than daytime accidents because your child didn't have much choice in the matter if he didn't wake up at all. Plus, everyone is obviously tired. Try to handle nighttime accidents with a calm, problem-solving perspective.

Attend to your child's emotional as well as physical needs. He may be embarrassed, confused, and unhappy waking up in wet pajamas and wet sheets. Reassure him that the accidents are isolated instances; they will not happen every night. Listen to his worries and help find solutions together.

No-Fault Strategies

Talk about the situation with your child. Does he feel like he has to pee during the night? Is he willing to get out of bed to potty at night? Make sure he is clear about what he should do. Add night lights, floor "runway" lights, or a nearby nighttime potty chair.

Review the nighttime potty options. Add an extra potty time before you go to bed and first thing in the morning. Would your child prefer calling for you in the middle of the night? Is this okay with you if it happens once a month? Would it help to keep a potty chair in his room for a short time?

Reconsider bedtime routines. Have you been more lenient lately about those late night potty reminders? Does he say he'll stop in the potty after reading his books and then falls asleep instead? Is he drinking more?

Evaluate daytime routines. Are you or your child busier lately? Is he adjusting to some new challenges? Maybe your child needs ten minutes of family time to just hang out together after dinner.

Reassure your child. This is a problem you'll conquer together. Let him know that he's not alone. If you are still worried, contact your pediatrician to eliminate possible medical concerns.

Find practical solutions to the immediate situation. If your child is sleeping in underpants and having infrequent accidents, you can minimize the inconvenience with a plastic mattress cover. Let him know that it's no big deal to wash the bedding, especially if it's once in a while. He feels bad enough waking up to an unexpected mess.

Waking up in a wet bed is very unpleasant and has no teaching value. If your child consistently has nighttime accidents, go back to nighttime pull-ups. It frees him from the pressure of mastering something that is temporarily beyond his ability. Explain to him that he can wear his underpants at night when he wakes up dry in the morning for a week, or two. By six years old, most children have the physical control needed for nighttime success. A visit to the pediatrician will help identify or rule out any medical concerns.

Potty training is often three steps forward and two steps back. Your role is to be a supportive potty partner. You are the one who understands the big picture through all the minor challenges and setbacks. Have faith in your child's growing ability. And keep recharging your positive, playful attitude so you can give him a boost whenever he needs it.

Nighttime Manipulation

Children learn quickly that parents will jump at the promise of potty success. Call it potty power. However, potty requests should not take priority over your bedtime routine. A request for "one more" and then "one more" should be answered with "last time." Nighttime potty training is about your child's ability to empty her bladder before bedtime and then wait until morning. An older child who needs to use the potty can take care of it without a lot of bedtime hoopla.

Establish a clear, consistent nighttime routine—one trip to the potty, never more than two. If your child calls your bluff and has an accident, clean it up calmly and return him to bed as quickly as possible. Resist the urge for any potty discussions at this time. Tomorrow night, watch your child's intake of liquids, stay with the bedtime routine, and remind your child that this is the last potty stop for the night. Therefore, he should let all the pee out now.

Your child may spend a few nights trying to engage you in a potty power play. The challenge will end when he is convinced that you mean what you say. The other scenario has you waiting for his bathroom calls for months.

Sleepovers

Potty training is not a prerequisite skill for a happy sleepover. If your child is comfortable at a relative's house or at a friend's house, he can have a successful sleepover. You just need good communication and a realistic plan.

Give your child's host an accurate description of his potty skills.

- Be completely honest with your child. If your child has accidents, don't let him talk you into believing he won't. He can go on the sleepover if he agrees to realistic conditions.

- Make a realistic plan. Do you need the host to be a hands-on potty helper? Does your child need to agree to nighttime pull-ups? Do you need to send along a plastic mattress cover or your child's sleeping bag?

- Be completely honest about what's required for success. If the host doesn't want to be responsible to give your child reminders, it is better to wait a few months or longer to find a more fitting sleepover host.
- Give it a try and have a backup plan just in case:
  - Prepare in your head—"If this doesn't work, I'm ready to give a great pep talk and we'll go to our favorite place for breakfast."
  - Arrange with your child—"If you have an accident, I'll pack extra pajamas and your friend's mom will wrap up your sleeping bag for you."
  - Discuss in advance with the host—"If you notice that my son is upset, please call me at any time. I'll be happy to pick him up."

If sleeping away from home is uncomfortable for your child, invite your child's friends to a sleepover at your house. Respect your child's preference to either be open and nonchalant about his potty skills or to be quiet and discreet. Discretion is fine, but be sure your child is getting positive messages in your home that nighttime accidents are normal.

- Talk to your child ahead of time if he wears nighttime pull-ups. Is he okay that his friends see his pull-ups or does he want to put them on privately?
- Create a positive nighttime potty routine. It is better to do your "mom act" than have your child pretend not to need his usual bathroom routine?
- Incorporate the games for middle-of-the-night trips to the bathroom.
- Design sleeping arrangements to fit the situation—plastic mattress covers, sleeping bags, camping cots, and a camping theme.

- Have an accident plan. Don't ask children to guess what they should do "if," especially in an emotionally sensitive situation. Tell them you are nearby and ready to help.
- Plan a response to teasing, just in case. You never know if another child might say something hurtful. Teach your child early that those hurtful words say more about the speaker than about him. Remind him of the truth that potty accidents are nothing to be ashamed of. Then, teach him to stand up for herself and to tell others to "stop saying hurtful words."

At home or away, nighttime potty learning often adds an extra emotional dimension potty training. Skills that came easily during the day are more difficult when your child is tired or cozy in a bed. New vulnerabilities surface when your child wakes up alone in a dark room. You are tired and may not be at your most playful, resourceful best. But you're almost to the finish line. Now isn't the time to sabotage your success. Rally your resilience. Your child is counting on you to light the way.

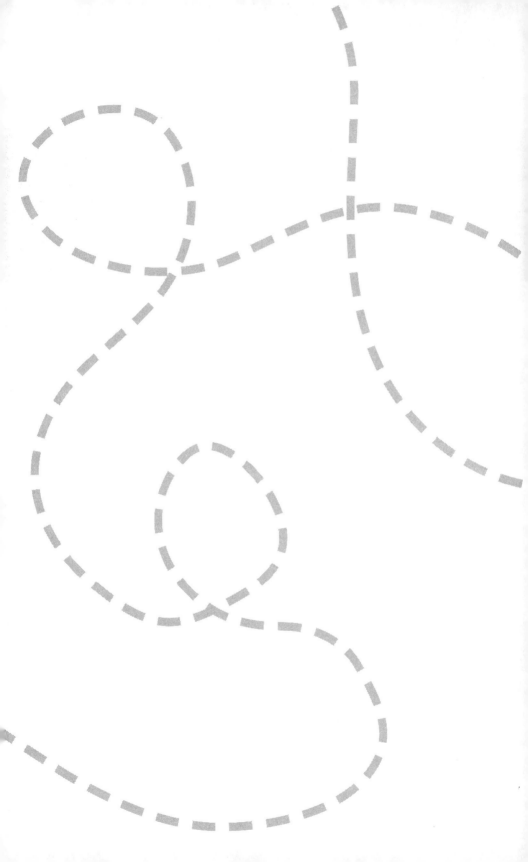

11

Positive Potty Solutions for Accidents, Fears, and Dilemmas

Your playful potty attitude is essential long after the potty play days of active potty training are finished. Although your child may be a successful potty goer at home under ideal circumstances, her potty skills will now be tested by a variety of real life situations. Some children will continue to be successful anywhere anytime. Others will need a supportive potty partner to help them to improvise those potty skills everywhere every time. Accidents happen. They are a normal and expected part of potty training.

Accidents can happen anytime your child is busy or distracted. Real life adds hundreds of distractions: an

Blame and humiliation are counterproductive in potty training. Negative emotions discourage future success and prevent your child from finding a better alternative. Your child still needs you as a supportive partner who is keeping her focused on her goal. You want your child to be a potty pro—resourceful when faced with the unexpected, motivated despite obstacles, and adaptable in imperfect conditions.

interesting video, a bug she's never seen before, or the last bite of a cookie. Young children have difficulty stopping whatever it is they are doing, even if everything is still waiting there when they return. It isn't rational, but it's the way children think.

Accidents can also happen when something is different than expected. Dad uses different words when he gives a potty reminder, the potty chair is in the wrong place, or your child is startled by the dog. She shifts her intellectual and emotional focus to comprehend the change—and whoops—she forgets what she seemed to know so well.

Potty-age children also frequently underestimate time. Accidents can happen because your child has an immature sense of time—she may underestimate how long it will take to finish something, how long it will take to get to the potty, or how long it will take to remove clothes.

The reasons for accidents are as numerous as hours in the day. Your child may be sick or in a bad mood. You may be sick or in a bad mood. Using the potty might seem such a bother today. Whatever the reason, accidents happen. Expect them.

Improv for Potty Accidents

Potty accidents are an opportunity for playful improvisation. Knowing there's no one right way to handle a potty situation can be a huge relief to you and to your child. Simply stay in the moment with her, listening and problem solving together. You'll be amazed at how much she learns when you turn negatives into positives. Potty improv teaches your child to acknowledge the unexpected and find a way to move forward.

Your child still needs you. She might need tangible help getting out of wet clothes or cleaning up a wet spot without making a bigger headache for you. She might just need to be held. No matter the situation, in this moment you are her point of reference for what to feel. When accidents happen, she learns to be sad, nervous, and ashamed or calm, creative, and in control based on your reaction.

In potty improv, you jump into your child's world and create a bridge from hers to yours. Watch. Listen. Read the situation. You can use the following three simple questions to advance your potty improvisation in difficult moments, either by asking your child directly or by using them to think through the next possible step.

- What should we do now?
- What do we need?
- Will that make it better?

> Sometimes a child might be embarrassed to return to the scene of a potty accident in a public place. Here is an opportunity to be a positive potty partner—lending a hand to hold or an encouraging word. Reassure your child that she will not be scolded or laughed at. Speak to any other adults involved to garner their support as well.

Most times the solution is the same: Clean your child and clean up the accident. The potty improv approach includes your child in the actual problem solving. When she is part of the problem solving, she is learning to be responsible, capable, and helpful without an emotional power struggle.

Let your child be part of the solution. It will teach her a sense of responsibility, just like when she wipes up spilt milk. Clean up together. Cleanup is not coercive or a form of punishment. Make cleanup a game, but be sure to let the grown-ups handle any actual poop cleanup.

- Keep it light. "Whoops, what should we do now? I think we have a cleanup here!"
- Ask for help. "I need a handy helper here! What do you think we need?"

- Make helping easy. Keep supplies (paper towels, a nontoxic cleaning solution, a change of clothes) in a child-accessible place (on a low shelf or in a basket in the bathroom).
- Lead the way. Start the cleanup if your child resists, acting as if she's a full participant. "We'll have this problem fixed in no time at all."
- Avoid long lectures. Let the natural consequence do the teaching for you. Only speak about "woulda, coulda, shoulda" if your child initiates it. Simply survey the situation: "Is our problem solved? Yep, looks good to me."
- Practice good hand washing afterwards.

When the solution isn't quite as obvious, especially in public places or when you're less prepared, pause for a moment. Sometimes, even an all-wise, all-knowing parent has no idea what to do. Here's your chance to be a truly great role model. When in doubt, stall. Just say, "Hmmm, I wonder what we should do now?" Let the world stop around you until you think of something. Improv with your child begins after you as the parent are back on solid ground.

> **Attend to your child's emotional needs as well as her physical needs. Reassure her that the accidents are isolated instances; they will not happen every time. Listen to her worries and help find solutions together.**

Improv also reminds you to have fun. Be silly! Remember to laugh, especially at yourself. But don't laugh at your child.

When Emotions Get in the Way

Many children have accidents after months of successful pottying. Remember, there are many reasons why your child is having accidents. She forgot. She got scared. She made a bad choice. After months of success, she is probably very aware of her mistakes.

Potty training is emotional and your child may have lost her previous sense of control.

Hold your emotions in check, particularly in front of your child. Continue to observe the situation for changes in your child's environment. If the situation doesn't improve, contact your pediatrician or speak to your child's teacher. But for now, wait and watch. Acknowledge the situation with acceptance and address the immediate problem—a change of clothes and a hand to hold. Reconfirm your faith in her ability.

Most of the time, your child's accidents are genuine mistakes. It is possible, however, that your child's behavior has become a "game," particularly if you have allowed your emotions to rule your reactions. When children learn that they can push parents' buttons, they are almost compelled to do so. It gives them power, albeit inappropriate power. They can pull you into an ever-escalating emotional drama. They get attention—they win, in child-logic anyway.

One sure way out of the game is to neutralize your emotional response. Take a grown-up time-out. Count to ten. Count to fifty. The game frequently happens during one of those oppositional stages in development when your child is strongly asserting his independence He is probably experimenting with your emotional reaction more so than his potty skills.

As much as you might like to, you cannot force your child to use the potty. Although you may be angry at your child's willfulness, the best long-term strategy is always to pull back from the struggle. By doing this, you will shorten the oppositional stand-off and be able to return to a more playful potty interaction. Playfulness always wins out over negative attention when volatile emotions are taken out of the drama.

Strategies for Power Struggles

Here are a few strategies to handle these normal developmental "testing" behaviors that spill over into the potty training process. Your potty-age child may not have the self-restraint to avoid escalating conflicts, so it's up to you to be the voice of calm. These power struggles pit you against your child at a time when your child needs respectful guidance on her side.

- Stay calm, at least while in the same room as your child. Try something like, "Instead of fighting, I'll be back in two minutes. Then we can figure this out."
- Let the "rules" speak, instead of your authority. For example, "Everyone has to wear a pull-up or underpants in the store. Which one will it be?"
- Substitute gentle reminders for harsh directives. Avoid statements like, "Put those pants on right NOW!" Instead, offer the choice, "Two more minutes to get your pants on and then I'll be in to help you."
- Do not give choices when you don't mean it. Instead of "Do you want to go potty before getting in the car?" try in a sing-songy voice, "Time for pre-car potty pit stop!"
- Give lots of empowering choices when you do mean it—when either choice leads your child to the desired behavior. For example, hop or skip to the bathroom? Superman or SpongeBob underwear?
- Shut down inappropriate "power surges" quickly. For example, if your child is ready to throw the potty chair, take it calmly and place it out of reach.
- Be ready to say what you want your child to do, not what you don't want. For example, "Let's relax and take a minute to regroup." Or, "We need to walk to our car. It's hard to think with so many people watching us."
- Expect more tantrums as your child releases excessive frustration. Have a tantrum plan to contain hurtful behavior—designate a place where your child can fall apart without hurting himself or being destructive.
- Power struggles are never fun. Just remember, testing behavior is a necessary part of healthy development—that is, when the parents don't fall apart, too.

Potty Reminders

After your potty play days, you'll gradually turn over the responsibility to remember to potty to your child. Of course, depending on your child, this transfer might be fast or slow. The best strategies to give your child ownership over her potty training experience are ones that keep your involvement as invisible as possible.

- Use routines. Create new habits for your child by incorporating potty stops into natural daily transition times. Routines are one reason why preschools are so successful at potty training. Everyone takes regular preventative potty breaks. What are the optimal times? When your child first wakes up, before she gets dressed, after breakfast, before all car trips, when you arrive in new places, and before beginning involved activities are all optimal potty times. Keep in mind that you can't force your child to potty. Never insist that she has to actually potty—only state matter-of-factly that these are times to "sit and try," just in case.
- Use signals. Children need gentle—as in non-nagging—reminders. Verbal reminders are fine, but feel free to be creative, too. Draw an imaginary "P" with a question mark on your child's back when you think it's been a while since her last potty break. Give a "T" hand signal for a potty time-out.
- Be silly. Ask your child to hop like a bunny or run like a cheetah to the bathroom. Count backwards from 10 and see if your child can "beat the clock." Pretend to fly, swim or be invisible.

What if you've given your child all the appropriate reminders and she's still dancing the potty two-step in the family room when she should be on her way to the bathroom? Let it be her accident. That might sound completely avoidable and unnecessary to you as an adult, but you already know how to use the potty. If you could make your child's potty choices, the potty training process would be infinitely easier. However, some children need to find out for themselves.

Maybe your child is playing a game with her body to see how long she can wait. Maybe she wishes she could play for five more minutes and then go. The situation will change as soon as your child doesn't like the outcome. Stay calm. Be patient. This problem won't last forever.

If your child is interested in using the potty but is too impatient to sit still, you may want to incorporate some fun delay tactics. Sing a song together, read a story, teach her to whistle—anything that will help your child to slow down. *The Fast Boy* story on page 105 was written just for this child! Playful potty training encourages you to work *with* your child's exuberance—not against it.

In the meantime, treat the accident like any other accident. Let her be aware of the near-miss and clean it up without too much fanfare. Her initial impulsiveness should not lead to deliberate carelessness. With more experience, she will learn to be more careful.

If your child starts to pee on the potty, then stops halfway through and finishes peeing in her pants, she may be less than 100 percent sold on the potty process. Watch for excessive external expectations. Let her wear pull-ups until she's more willing to use the potty. She may need more time to become a trusting friend of the potty.

The Diaper Dilemma

Sometimes a child who knows how to use the potty will ask for a diaper now and then. How you handle this situation is directly related to your potty training personality. Can you be flexible without losing faith? Can you introduce a little inconsistency without confusing your child? Can you say "No" while still acknowledging her underlying need?

Try to understand what lies behind her request. Is there a new sibling in the house? Is your child having doubts about growing up? Is this a request for attention or for reassurance? Attention without reassurance will lead to more requests for attention and escalate the situation. Attention with reassurance will meet your child's needs and allow her to continue to move forward.

Choose the response that feels right to you:

- Say "Okay, just this one special time." Have a follow-up conversation with your child. "Why" questions are difficult for three-year-olds to answer, so try to explore the situation in other ways. Instead ask, "How does it feel to wear the diaper again?" "Do you want a break from thinking about the potty?"

- Use humor and play to redirect the situation without laughing at your child. For example, "I don't have any more diapers. Let's make pretend diapers out of paper towels and put them on your teddy bears."

- Address the need in other ways. Sometimes it's not about the diapers but the ambiguity of growing up. Validate the need with simple words like, "I loved it when you were a baby and I took care of you all the time. Let's plan some special time for just you and me." Then add a morning snuggle time together, time each day to look at baby pictures, take an evening walk, or go on a Saturday afternoon ice cream outing.

Improv for Potty Fears

Fears are a normal part of childhood. Fears might be small isolated moments when your child is face-to-face with something unfamiliar. Sometimes all your child needs is a familiar context. "Hey, this toilet looks different than ours. But look at all the ways it's also the same as the one in our bathroom." A simple explanation, a helpful suggestion, or a hand to hold might be all your child needs to move forward. Rational support can help in situations where the fears are specific and clear.

Other times, fears are deep and developmental. The potty training years coincide with a time of sweeping, yet normal, emotional growth. The deepest fear may not be the toilet at all. It may be the more developmental struggle with separation. Separation struggles recur all through childhood as your child grows slowly and steadily into a person. Your child cannot calmly say, "I'm afraid if I fall in that big toilet, I'll slip into the drain and never see you again." Or, as one three-year-old told her mother after weeks of distress, "I want to wear my diaper to bed because I don't want to get old and die."

Never dismiss a fear as trivial or nonsense. Your child's fear may not be rational to you as an adult but it always adheres to the standards of child-logic. You may not know where it originates. It may contradict good sense. But it is real to your child.

Every fear is an opportunity. In potty improv, you are making a guess at a likely solution and waiting to see if your child picks up on it. Whenever possible, let your child decide what to do.

> **Routines and rituals help transform the unknown into something safe and predictable. Your child is no longer a small person in an out-of-control situation. Your child is the master of her world.**

Present your child with a few options. You can offer tangible help by saying "Would you like a hand to hold? I won't let you fall in the toilet." Or you can employ a little improv magic, such as "Would you like these fairy wings to hold you up while you sit on the potty? I have some right here in my pocket." Sometimes she just needs a new direction. Then, she can conquer the fear alone. Sometimes, she's willing to act but needs the physical reassurance that she is not alone. Other times, you will have to act for her while she watches her brave and resourceful role model.

In order to potty improv through a fearful situation, you must think like your child. Here are a few examples of how you might guide your child through typical potty fears. Improv situations move forward with "yes, and . . ." Start with the fear, then continue with "yes, and . . ." Consider the situation. "What should we do? What do we need? Will that make it better?" The examples in this chapter give suggestions for one possible "and" but you and your child can go in any number of directions. It's called improv because your child's participation shapes the ultimate solution. By listening and watching your child's response, you get closer to the heart of the fear and arrive at a solution together.

The Move from a Potty Chair to a Full Size Toilet

Help your child put the problem in words. You might say, "You're right. The toilet is bigger than your little potty chair. What should we do now?" Talk about everyday things that are big and small. Make this a math puzzle. Add a little humor. "Do little bottoms fit on big toilets? Oh no . . . do big bottoms fit on little potties?" Think to yourself or ask your child "What do we need?" Get dramatic. "What do we do if a little bottom falls into a big toilet? We might scream! We might cry! We might say heeeeeelp!" If your child is verbal, all this talking might help her take control of her experience. Think or ask "Does that make it better?" If not, try other approaches next time.

> Potty training is an emotional accomplishment as much as it is a physical accomplishment. Addressing fears as they arise will teach your child potty flexibility and all important adaptability. It's big world out there, and it's full of potties.

For some children, talking about the toilet won't be enough. You will need a more emotional response. Build confidence slowly. Add an emotional dimension to your problem solving. Use a doll or teddy bear to rehearse the experience. Explore fears through pretend play. If teddy falls in and gets a wet bottom, show your child how you will hold him and comfort him.

Fear of Flushing

Plenty of children have fears about flushing the toilet. No wonder—there's noisy, swirling water that whisks everything away never to be seen again. It's fast, efficient, and inexplicable. And that's without mentioning that what it takes away is something the child "made." Flushing is scary.

Start by trying to verbalize the source of your child's fear. Choose your words and watch your child's body language. You'll see her body relax a little when you get it right. For example: "Get ready, here comes the LOUD flushing sound." Or "Round and round the water goes, until the bowl is empty at last." Or "You don't like that flusher, do you?"

Think or ask "What should we do now?" Try to find the least disruptive solution. Will your child watch as you flush the toilet? Is it easier if she doesn't watch the contents empty? If so, make it a game to close the toilet lid, say "abracadabra," and then check to see if everything is gone. Now think or ask "What do we need?" A magic wand or a little time and distance? Or, simply explain that you see that flushing scares her so you will flush it later, no problem. Now evaluate: Did that make it better? You might even talk about how scary it is in neutral settings, while on a walk or while riding in the car. Tell stories and pretend to flush the toilet over and over. Visit the water treatment plant to understand the mystery of where the poop goes.

The Automatic Flusher

Public auto-flush toilets create a new set of fear-inspired drama. Begin by acknowledging this fear: "*Yes*, that's scary *and*. . . ." What can we do to minimize the surprise? Make it your public potty routine to check stalls for auto-flush features. Again, potty-age children love high drama. Think or ask, "What do we need?"

Assume a John Wayne posture and a tough-guy voice, "Okay, we're coming in and we're not afraid of you flushers." Pretend to shine a flush-checking flashlight, "I know you're there and I know when you're going to flush." Keep your child engaged in the power play. Then, help her to prepare for the auto-flush. Talk to the evil flusher, "okay flusher, no flushing until I'm ready. I'm counting: one, two, three." Did that make it better? Your child is learning first-hand to be brave in the face of her fear.

Pooping in the Toilet

Sometimes a child will have all the other potty training skills but still ask for a diaper or a pull-up to poop. *Yes*, the diaper or pull-up allows your child to relax, that emotional security is essential when pooping. Ask yourself, "What should we do now?" You can try to empty the poop from the diaper into the toilet and let your child participate in the rest of the potty routine: wiping, flushing, hand washing. Reassure your child with a positive message that "one day she'll be ready to poop in the toilet like mommy and daddy" and to let you know when she wants to try. Did that make it better?

If your child is feeling like a part of her body is falling

> **Your child has more likelihood for success if surrounded by clear, consistent potty messages. Throwing up your hands in frustration while saying, "I quit. This isn't worth it!" is not an option. Calmly saying to your child, "I don't want to fight about pottying. We'll try again another time" is acceptable. The first gives your child mixed messages. The second is a mutually acceptable time-out.**

off or being taken away to a mysterious place, she needs more time to comprehend the process. *Yes, and* "What should we do now?" Take baby steps? Could we make a game of listening for the poop to fall into the water or use your other "potty games" like telling stories? One insightful dad knew his daughter was fearful about the poop plopping and splashing. So he reenacted the sensation by dropping candy kisses into the toilet. What will make it better for your child in this situation? Your child will give you the answer if you playfully enter her child-centered world.

Of course, the reason for the problem might be a physical difficulty with pooping while sitting on the toilet. Be sure your child can plant her feet firmly on the ground; otherwise, she may be having difficulty pushing the poop out.

"Withholding" Poop

Some children get "stuck." They don't want to poop in the pull-up but they are still frightened by the alternatives. Unfortunately, getting emotionally "stuck" can lead to getting physically stuck. Potty training is not fun when your child is constipated. Do not give your child over-the-counter laxatives or medicines without the approval of your pediatrician.

Instead, you can use potty improv to get your child "unstuck." First ask, "What should we do now?" Be silly. Look in her tummy with your special X-ray poop glasses. Did that make it better? Sometimes you can complement the improv strategies with other non-improv solutions. Give your child more choices in other areas to

> Younger children who are "making friends" with the potty may sit on the potty for quite a while, looking at books or checking out how their new chair feels. Once your child is in the habit of using the potty, there's no reason for her to sit there if nothing is happening. This could be a signal to ask if your child feels constipated or has other uncomfortable feelings. Don't rush your child, but don't let her sit there all day, either.

boost her need for constructive control: what she wears, what books she reads, what characters are on the bathroom towels. Keep potty experiences positive while you try to create more relaxing conditions: add poop-friendly foods, simplify your child's daily schedule, make potty trips easy and unthreatening, and conclude each day with a quiet snuggle time when you reestablish an unconditional connection with your child.

Explain that you don't want her to hold in the poop because it can make her sick and it hurts her body. With positive potty conditions and your relaxed support, your child will trust her body again.

With each potty situation, keep improvising until your child is ready to move forward. She has an inner clock that announces when enough is enough. Your child needs the freedom to pretend until she has the confidence to proceed without pretending. She needs the flexibility to practice new skills until they become automatic. And she needs the privilege of repeating questions and mistakes. Mistakes are merely evidence that there's still more to learn.

At the same time, you will become a master at improv in any situation. While you once jumped into your child's world when she had a problem, your goal is now to lead her into the shared world of family and friends. You will live with one foot in each world: the "real" world and your child's world. You'll know you've been a successful potty partner when you have bridged these two worlds. Now you can enjoy making improv part of your ongoing parenting repertoire.

Talking to Your Child about Potty Problems

Potty-age children do not always know the right words to express emotions and problems. They have difficulty expressing themselves when they are confused, frustrated, or overwhelmed. You can feel like you're playing a guessing game—is it this or is it that? You might feel increasingly anxious if the situation concerns a change in your child's potty habits or a fear about a talk about a potty situation. Start by setting up good listening conditions and then help your child find the words that fit her needs. Children's concerns tend to percolate up at unexpected quieter times.

- Create listening times throughout the day when your child has your full attention—in the car, on walks, on a swing, at bedtime.
- Lead with open-ended statements—"I noticed you needed a change of clothes at school today."
- Create a supportive environment for any possible answer, from "I hate school" to "You're stupid."
- Respond to feelings, not merely to words—"Sounds like it was a rough day" or "I can help when you want to tell me about it."
- Don't rush—stay available to finish the conversation when your child is ready.
- Collect accurate information from other sources and tell your child what you think is happening—"The doctor says you need some medicine to help you poop. I want you to tell me when it hurts so I can help make it better."

Listening is often as important as problem solving. Keep in mind that talking about potty situations might be all that is needed for your child to process the situation on her own.

As your child's world grows larger and larger, she may need to talk to other adults such as relatives and teachers about potty problems. Your child may need your help learning to speak up for what she needs in a timely way. Even kindergartners can struggle with this. Here are some tips for helping your child speak up to other adults:

- Encourage your child to speak up at home. Resist the urge to read her mind just to save time. Verbalizing potty needs is an essential skill.

- Practice speaking up with different adults that your child knows. A child might hesitate to speak up because an adult looks or acts differently. A teacher might have different glasses or a quirky smile. Sometimes adults appear gruff or rushed when in fact they are willing to help.

- Rehearse speaking with puppets or practicing with you. Be sure to let your child "play" herself and "play" the role of the other person.

- Be a positive role model. Let your child see you talking with the person. If the other person isn't a good listener, demonstrate how to catch that person's attention.

> **Your potty trained child's curiosity might be tempted by the extra bathroom time. Check your bathroom door locks before your child realizes he can lock you out. Turn the handle around so the lock is on the outside of the door—that way, no one can get locked in.**

- Speak up yourself. When you drop off your child in a new setting, let the other person know that your child needs some extra encouragement with this new skill.

Health Concerns

Your pediatrician is a wonderful resource and ally on your potty training team, with a wealth of medical and developmental information. Contact your pediatrician whenever you need reassurance to the eternal parenting question, "Is this normal?" Sometimes, you just need to ask. Don't struggle and worry alone.

Successful potty training requires many behavioral, social, and emotional skills. It also requires a healthy body. You know your child's body better than you know your own. Contact your pediatrician whenever you have questions about your child's health.

- Contact your pediatrician any time your child's potty habits change:
    - If your child is constipated
    - If your child starts having regular wetting accidents after months of success
    - If you notice small leaks regularly on underwear
- Contact your pediatrician if you notice changes in your child's pee or poop:
    - Color (not food related)
    - Odors
    - Blood
    - Too hard or too soft
- Contact your pediatrician any time you suspect it's painful for your child to pee or to poop.
- Contact your pediatrician anytime your child shows unexplainable physical distress:
    - Fever
    - Vomiting
    - Refusal to eat
    - Lethargy
    - Abdominal or back pain
- Contact your pediatrician for bed wetting after the age of five or six.

Teaching Potty Etiquette

Social Situations

Once your child is interested in potty training, you might hear her interviewing everyone she sees about their potty preferences—strangers in grocery lines and grandparents included. Everyone in earshot will soon learn what's on your child's learning agenda. Be prepared during the potty training process to discuss seemingly private topics in the most unusual places. That's a good sign you're doing the right thing.

You can begin to teach the nuances of social etiquette by redirecting the conversation. Simply explain to others that your child is excited about potty training. Social graces are best taught by example at this age. Young children do not understand that potty training might not be a proper topic at the holiday dinner table.

Similarly, if your child wants to show others her private body parts, remind her that she should wait until she gets into the bathroom to take off her clothes. Validate her enthusiasm for the new things she is learning and add this to the list of "everything in its place" principle of potty training.

A "Potty" Mouth

Your child is the master of the bathroom and of her body. She has also learned the power of potty words—poopy head, pee-pee breath, penis face, and every combination thereof. The words have power because children laugh and adults go wild. The behavior is all about attention. As soon as you remove the pay-off, the behavior will disappear.

As always, remove the emotional incentive. Your child has the power if she knows she is pushing your buttons. It is better for her to discover that power through her other positive abilities. Speak calmly and directly, "I don't like those words." If your child continues, remove the audience. Leave the scene or separate the children. Again, explain what you're doing, "We aren't going to listen to you." Or ""We'll be back when you're done being silly."

Calm and direct always works. There are some situations, however, when your child isn't sure you mean what you say. In these cases, the provocative behavior escalates. Stay calm. Your child is just checking you.

Of course, you are human. If your first reaction was to hush, scold, and threaten, that's normal. Just take three steps backward—admit that you lost it, explain again calmly what behavior is appropriate, and change the immediate situation. Let it be—there's no need to repeat your point until your child winds up for a second round.

Peeing Contests

Whether it's Freud or testosterone, boys discover quickly that penises can pee near and far, in lines and in circles, on walls or on snow. This gets to be a problem when you realize your child has inadvertently crossed your comfort boundary. While your child's actions begin as spontaneous and innocent, they can quickly pass the line of what you consider appropriate.

Teach your child appropriate behaviors early—what's okay outside but not inside, what's okay in the back yard but not in the front yard, what's okay at home with dad but not at school or at friends' houses.

- Know your child. Your boundaries might be realistic or unrealistic. Keep the rules simple if you think your child will have difficulty remembering them.
- Know the power of peers. Expect the laughter and attention of peers to outweigh the most sensible rules.
- Know the principle of escalating action. Some actions are so completely self-satisfying that they assume their own momentum. Know when to stop and when to continue before behavior gets out of control.

Playing with Poop

Why would a child play with poop? Because it's there. Plus, she has yet to learn all of the negative associations that you have. It's gross, but so are boogers and spit balls. Gross isn't much of a deterrent to children.

If your child discovers the playful qualities of poop, be prepared to be extra watchful in the days and weeks ahead. Poop may have a self-reinforcing attraction to your child—it's soft and squishy and smears well. An emotional response on your part ("Ooooh gross," "Stop, that's disgusting," or "Yuuuuuuuck") also reinforces the behavior. It could create a greater interest to play with poop.

Stay calm in front of your child. Scream, laugh, or cry with your potty-support friends. Describe the problem: "Poop belongs in the potty. It has germs. So, we don't touch it with our hands. And that's why we wash our hands every time we use the potty." Fix the problem: "Let's clean this up." No scolding is necessary if you clearly present what is and what is not okay to do with poop. Because poop may hold a unique attraction to your child, allow for the possibility that this is not a one-time experience. You may have to repeat your message a few more times.

End with a positive. If your child loves to get messy or loves oooey, gooey textures, incorporate more of those things into her play. Try squishing Play-Doh, finger painting with paint or pudding, mixing a bowl of flour with a pitcher of water, digging in the garden, or making mud pies.

Public Bathrooms

Family restrooms and single-toilet bathrooms make parents' lives much easier. Both parents can co-parent, venturing separately into the world with their children.

When faced with a men's room and a ladies' room, however, moms have a distinct advantage. Since the baby changing stations are in the women's rest room, moms with little boys can do what they always did—bring boys into the ladies' room. If a mom wants her son to experience the urinal in the men's bathroom, she should go into the bathroom with her child. It's probably best to announce your entrance before coming through the door, "Mom coming in!"

Dads can do the same when entering a ladies' bathroom, "Dad coming in!" More typically, dads are taking daughters into the men's room. Rumor has it that men's rooms might not be as clean and potty-friendly as the ladies' rooms. You might consider packing your child's backpack with sanitizing wipes, toilet seat covers, or a travel potty seat. Some dads choose to avoid the decision altogether and carry a travel potty.

Young children should not go into public bathrooms without supervision. Although your child might enjoy the freedom of pottying on her own, that doesn't mean she is old enough to be alone in a public bathroom. Young children do not have the cognitive skills to predict negative consequences, and they cannot know the risks inherent in certain decisions. Even when children have been taught safety routines, they are easily distracted and persuaded to act otherwise. Adults, not children, are responsible for keeping children safe. Besides, if they go into a bathroom alone, who will be there to watch your child's hand washing?

If you happen to be in a non-child-friendly place, be prepared to neutralize negative stares and whispers with simple comments that your child can understand. "Yes, we had an accident and we're doing a good job of fixing the problem."

There is no reason not to accompany your child into a public bathroom. However, if you choose to wait outside a public bathroom door for your child, create a bathroom game that keeps you in contact with your child. Play "daddy echo," repeating silly things that your child says or an alphabet/counting game where each one of you says the next letter/number. If time runs out and you're on a busy city street, you may not have many options. Do whatever you can to minimize your child's discomfort and to make cleanup as easy as possible.

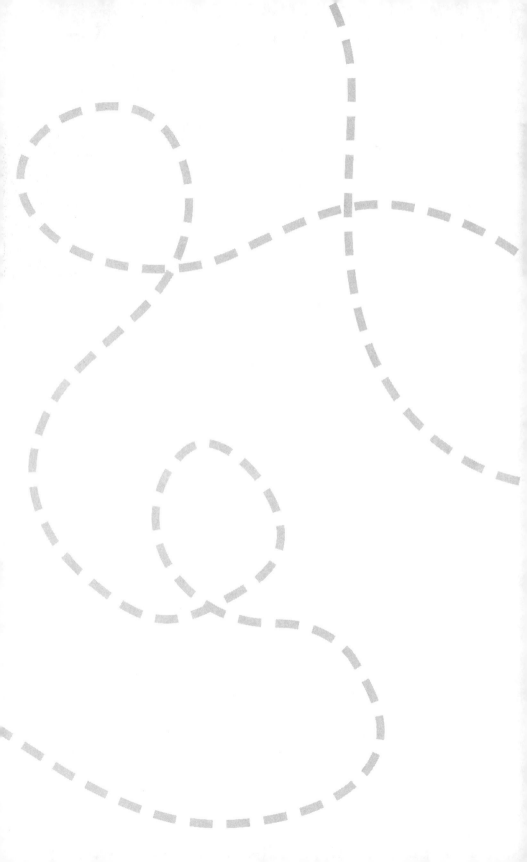

Congratulations

Hooray, you did it! You managed to go through potty training with a sense of play and a sense of humor. You empowered your child to grow in powerful ways by showing him control of his body, his choices, and his actions.

Potty training brings together body, mind, and emotions at a time when your child is becoming an independent person. He is now in control of his body and is capable of taking care of an important physical need every day. He can enjoy the pride of his accomplishment. You, meanwhile, can enjoy a newfound freedom from diapers.

Continue to support a healthy connection between your child's body and mind. Your child learned his body is predictable and gives him clear signals about what it needs. Build on your child's awareness that he knows his body. Whether he's tired, hungry, or sleepy, let him "read" his body just like he does when he needs to potty. Guide him to choices that will honor his body. Then, he will grow up knowing that his body and his mind work together to make him happy and healthy.

Potty training might have been easy or challenging. Either way, your child learned about learning. He mastered a complex skill that leads the way to new freedom and independence. He learned to take responsibility for his needs and her actions. He learned to trust others to guide him to good choices and to ask for help when he needs it. He learned to take a few risks in new situations, that it was better to take a risk and make a mistake than to take no risk at all. He learned that learning eventually leads to success.

In retrospect, he is both the same child you held in your arms a few years ago and a different child who has new needs and abilities. Every time your child passes a new developmental milestone, he grows. Most of all, your child learned he is smart, capable, and loved.

Potty training is an important milestone in your child's development. Potty training is also a huge milestone in the stages of parent development. Much has been written about parent-infant bonding, but you just went through an extraordinary dance of mutual cooperation. When your child was an infant, you tuned into his likes, dislikes, and needs, large and small. You anticipated how to make him happy and minimize his distress and discomfort. You created a world of love and belonging just for him.

In potty training you did the same dance, but this time your child was an active partner. You learned your child's strengths and your child's limits. You taught your child to trust those strengths and to face those limits—to use one and to rise above the other. You created a potty training world for your child to try, to fail, and to succeed. You learned when to lead and when to follow. Potty training is a success that you share with your child.

In every case, you also learned something about yourself as a parent. You may have discovered a few unknown strengths—resilience, humor, patience—along with a few personal limits—frustration, confusion, despair. But you grew with your child. You are not exactly the same person you were when you began this potty adventure, but you are definitely better equipped for the next stage of parenting. There may have been some stressful moments along the way. You may have even made a few mistakes.

But now you know those were merely times to learn a little more. You are now far better equipped for any future parenting situation. You understand your child better and you know how to be a teacher as well as a playful partner.

Most importantly, your child did it. Hooray! Your child can be proud of himself. He mastered a complex skill that leads the way to new freedom and independence. He learned to take responsibility for his needs and his actions. He learned to trust others to guide him to good choices and to ask for help when he needs it. He learned to take a few risks in new situations, and that it was better to take a risk and make a mistake than to take no risk at all. Most of all, your child learned he is smart, capable, and loved.

Keep playing!

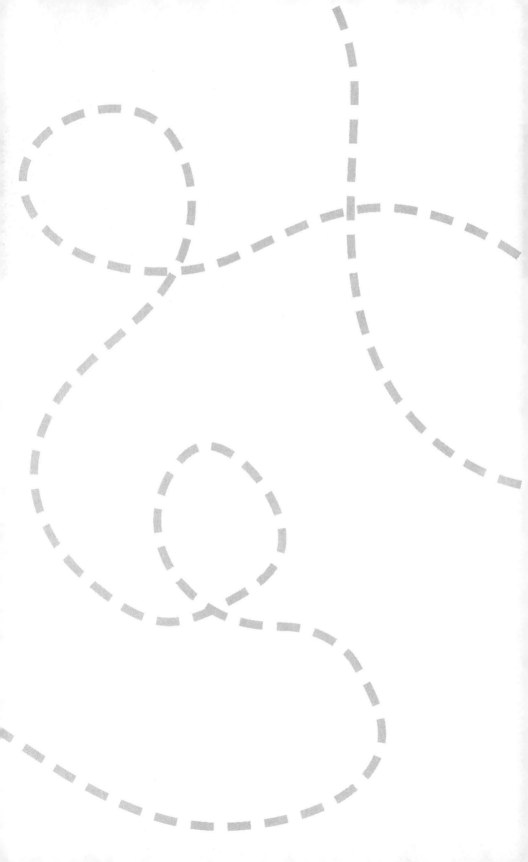

Appendix A: Potty Books, Videos, and Stories

Popular Children's Potty Books

A Potty for Me! by Karen Katz

Does a Pig Flush? by Fred Ehrlich

Everyone Poops by Taro Gomi

Go, Girl! Go Potty! by Harriet Ziefert Inc.

Going to the Potty by Fred Rogers

I Have to Go! by Robert Munsch

Lift the Lid, Use the Potty by Annie Ingle and Lisa McCue

No More Diapers for Ducky by Bernette Ford and Sam Williams

No Potty! Yes, Potty! by Harriet Ziefert Inc.

Once Upon a Potty by Alona Frankel

The Prince and the Potty by Wendy Cheyette Lewison

The Princess and the Potty by Wendy Cheyette Lewison

The Potty Book for Boys by Alyssa Satin Capucilli

The Potty Book for Girls by Alyssa Satin Capucilli

Time to Pee by Mo Willems

Uh Oh! Gotta Go! Potty Tales from Toddlers by Bob McGrath

What Do You Do with a Potty? by Marianne Borgardt

Where's the Poop? by Julie Markes and Susan Kathleen Hartung

You Can Go to the Potty by William Sears, MD, Martha Sears, RN, and Christie Watts Kelly
Your New Potty by Joanna Cole

Homemade Potty Books and Stories

My Potty Book—a personal "how to" potty chronicle
My Two Houses—a visual comparison of "new" and "old" potties
My World of Potties—a pictorial study of various toilets and potties
Underwear and Diapers—a book of friends and family and what they wear

Oral Storytelling

Fast Boy—the story of the child who can't sit still
Growing Every Day—the story of changing from a baby to a child
My Body and Me—the explanation of a child's body and feelings

Underwear Books

Arthur's Underwear by Marc Brown
Underwear! by Mary Elise Monsell and Lynn Munsinger
What Color Is Your Underwear? by Sam Lloyd

Favorite Children's Potty Videos

Bear in the Big Blue House by Martin Hugh Mitchell
I Can Go Potty by Mazzarella Productions
It's Potty Time by Learning Through Entertainment, Inc.
Let's Go Potty by Dr. Betti Hertzberg
Once Upon a Potty for Her by Alona Frankel
Once Upon a Potty for Him by Alona Frankel

Appendix B: Potty Songs, Rhymes, and CDs

Children's Potty Songs and Music

Ants by Joe Scruggs ("Big Underwear")

Miss Joanie's Potty Party by Joanie Whittaker

The Once Upon a Potty—Potty Songs CD by Ari Frankel

Potty Animal: Funny Songs about Potty Training by Auntie Poo & The Porta-Potties

Potty Song: Customized Potty Training Song at www.pottysong.com

Potty Song 1, Potty Song 2, and Potty Song 3 (free potty songs) on www.pottytrainingconcepts.com

Tinkle, Tinkle, Little Tot: Songs and Rhymes for Toilet Training (book) by Bruce Lansky, Robert Pottle, and Friends

Improvised Potty Songs

Happy Potty Song (Tune: "Happy Birthday")

Happy potty to me.

Happy potty to me.

I'm learning where to pee.

Happy potty to me!
Happy potty to me.
Happy potty to me.
I'm learning where to poopie.
Happy potty to me!

This Is the Way (Tune: "Here We Go 'Round the Mulberry Bush")

This is the way we sit on the potty,
Sit on the potty, sit on the potty,
This is the way we sit on the potty,
Early in the morning.
(every afternoon/early in the ev'ning/before we go to bed)

Are You Peeing? (Tune: "Frere Jacques")

Are you peeing? Are you peeing?
Little one? Little one?
Yes, I am. Yes, I am.
Now I'm done. Now I'm done.

Bathroom Clean-Up Song (Tune: "Old McDonald")

Substitute your child's name for David
Little David cleaned the mess.
E-I-E-I-O.
With a wipe wipe here and a wipe wipe there.
E-I-E-I-O.
Little David cleaned the mess.
E-I-E-I-O.
Additional Verses:
Little David sprayed the spray.
Little David wiped the floor.
Little David pitched the trash.

Appendix C:
Potty Training Games

Potty Time Signals

Draw a "P" with a question mark on your child's back.
Give a "T" hand signal for a potty time-out.
Set fun buzzers or timers.

Sitting on the Potty Games

Whistle while you wait.
Play "I spy."
Play "I hear."
Customize your own "Fast Boy" story.

Happy Successes

Potty tallies on a bathroom whiteboard or chalkboard
Happy faces on the bathroom mirror
Bathroom bell ringing

Mini-celebrations with cupcakes and a potty candle-lighting ceremony

A photo wall of happy potty pictures

Phone calls with positive potty reports to friends and relatives

"Red light" and "green light" cards

"High Five" wall poster

Toilet paper rolls for your child to "toot her horn"

Grand Finale Rituals

Dance around a trash can as you throw away the last diaper.

Throw an underwear party and have everyone wear silly underwear over their clothes, fly underwear flags, and invite friends and family to an underwear parade where they will be waving underwear on sticks.

Appendix D:
Potty Training Resources

Potty Training Supplies

Potty seats and chairs
Potty toppers
Potty training car seat liners
Step stools
Potty training pants and covers
Potty training dolls
Potty training charts and stickers
Potty training games and calendars
Potty time watches
Potty targets
Potty training urinals
Flushable potty clothes and wipes
Toilet paper for children
Mattress pads and covers
Night lights and toilet lights
Velcro easy-off belts
Potty travel mitts

Auto-flush stoppers
Potty training cleaning supplies

Potty Resource Websites

www.babycenter.com
www.babylove.com
www.babiesrus.com
www.companystore.com
www.pottytrainingconcepts.com
www.pottytrainingsolutions.com
www.onestepahead.com

Index

D

E

About the Author

Karen Deerweester is the owner of Family Time Coaching & Consulting in South Florida and is a highly requested speaker and trainer for parents and educators. Karen reaches millions of parents each month as the parenting expert for Bluesuitmom.com, as the author of the Toddler/Preschooler Column for *South Florida Parenting Magazine*, and through her writing on numerous parenting websites. She has appeared on MSNBC, as well as in *Parents* and *Parenting* magazines. Her popular parenting CD entitled *Parenting Quick Tips for Young Children* was featured in the premier issue of Dr. Phil's magazine, *The Next Level*.